Teaching Our Children to Pray

by Susan L. Lingo

STANDARD
PUBLISHING
Cincinnati, Ohio

Edited by Henrietta Gambill
Designed by Bob Korth

Art by Dina Sorn and Michael Streff

The Standard Publishing Company, Cincinnati, Ohio
A division of Standex International Corporation

With heart
filled love to
Clive, Dane
and Lindsay,
God's loving
answers
to prayer.

Dispelling the Prayer Myth

"You never teached me how!"

Michael, age 4

As parents, we've assumed the myth that prayer is an innate ability; that the birth of our child ushers in a quality prayer life. We ask our children to say their prayers, yet we do not teach them how. We encourage them to speak with God, yet we never share why or what God promises us when we do. We take so much for granted; leave too much unsaid.

Let's open our Bibles and take a hard look at perhaps the most important chapter on prayer the entire Book contains: Luke 11:1-14. As this chapter opens, the twelve disciples are listening intently as Jesus prays to his Father. Now, prayers were not something new that Jesus began. In fact, our earliest reference to the power of prayer is back in Genesis 4:26 when Seth and his family began to call upon the name of the Lord. But as the disciples observed Jesus' prayer time with the Father, they saw and heard something wonderfully moving and powerfully complete in his prayers. They recognized and felt the lack in their own prayers. What was lacking in their prayers was fully evident in the words of Jesus, and they asked Jesus to teach them how to pray. It's important to notice that they asked Jesus to teach them how to pray.

Teaching prayer is not only a great concept, it's purely biblical. Imagine Jesus' joyous heart as his beloved disciples hungered to draw nearer to their Father through prayer. And what was Jesus' reply to their plea? Was it, "No, my beloved, prayer cannot be taught. It does not need to be taught." Absolutely not!

Rather, his reply has become the most cherished of biblical prayers: the Lord's Prayer. But even more important than the words Jesus spoke, was the prayer model he provided; one we will look at in more depth shortly. What is key in Luke 11:1 is the fact that powerful, faithful, strengthening prayer must be taught, and there is no better time than this very moment to begin to teach our children to pray with the full heart and authority Jesus grants them!

How can we understand the intricacies of finance and investments if we are only shown a dollar bill? Or do we feel all the stirring emotions of committed love by merely holding a paper heart? How then can we expect our children to deeply grasp the promises, power, and full love of God with a quick grace at dinnertime? We must physically, emotionally, and spiritually teach them of God's faithfulness to hear and answer prayer; that with the authority Jesus entrusts to each of us, healing and intercession are to be nurtured as well as the two-way communication between God and our children that will drive them to seek the Father's strengthening love in their greatest times of need.

Consider for a moment how many little childhood prayers you may recall from the mists of your own past. Family grace around the dinner table or bedtime prayer ritual repeated word for word each night at 8 o'clock sharp. Typically, we pass down our own prayer styles and offer our children favorite rote prayers from our childhood, some of which are poor prayer models at best and no prayer

> ### "Now I lay me down to sleep . . ."
>
> **traditional bedtime prayer**

models at worst. How sad it is that we limit and may stifle our children's prayer spontaneity by teaching only the prayers that are traditional and familiar to us.

Would you rejoice over the gift of someone else's worn out socks when you were really hoping for their heart? So it must be with the Lord when he truly desires your child's deepest heartfelt prayers and receives instead the rote recitation of someone else's prayer. This brings us to a serious question: Is the rote prayer you have taught your child to recite really a prayer at all? Let's take a brief look at a classic childhood prayer through the eyes of a child to illustrate this point.

"Now I lay me down to sleep . . ."
"Okay so far, Mommy. It is bedtime and I am sleepy and happy."

"I pray the Lord my soul to keep."
"Who is the Lord, Mommy? What is his name, and why am I letting him keep something that belongs to me? What is my soul? I don't want to give it away, whatever it is."

"If I should die before I wake . . ."
"Die? I'm afraid I will die if I go to sleep. Will I see you again, Mommy? I don't want to die."

"I pray the Lord my soul to take."
"Please don't leave yet, Mommy! I don't want him to take anything from me! Please don't turn off the lights yet!"

Is this an overreaction? Not at all. These are very common thoughts that may run through your little one's mind when she says her prayers. It is important to understand that a young child literally visualizes what you, as an adult, are able to symbolically comprehend. To a little one, this prayer offers little, if any, comfort for the long, dark night ahead. What message are we instilling about the Lord and prayer time? That it is to raise concerns or to put them at ease? And even going beyond the actual message in the words, what about the rote repetition offered up? Each night the same words, the same tone of voice, the same time of day—rote, repetitious, dull, and cold.

Imagine coming to your best friend each day and repeating the identical things you said yesterday and the day before. After a few such repetitions, your friend would no doubt offer you a strong vitamin supplement for your failing memory and also feel genuine hurt that you were no longer sharing your innermost feelings. How much more must God grieve when a rote prayer is offered than a prayer from the heart—a prayer that's sparkling new and shiny each time we come before him. If God's constancy is the only unchanging aspect in our spiritual life, then our changing is the only sure part of our earthly existence. Our children's needs and emotions change daily, even hourly, and so must their prayers change to reflect sincerely open, honest hearts before God.

Rote prayer is not prayer at all. Have your children been starving upon this prayer diet? Then read on!

> "Our Father which art in heaven ..."
>
> Matthew 6:9-13, KJV

Five Fingers of Prayer

Jesus offered all of us a beautiful gift when he taught his disciples that first lesson in prayer so long ago. Through the Lord's Prayer, Jesus gives us the perfect **prayer model** containing the **5 Fingers of Prayer.** And it is with these blessed fingers that our children may go from "palm to palm" to "heart to heart" with their heavenly Father! Instead of rote prayer containing hollow words, we can use the stirring model that Jesus gave us to fashion our own words of prayer—words that are custom made, personally offered and containing the essence of what Jesus gave us in the Lord's Prayer. Here are the **5 Fingers of Prayer** and how they work to create the perfect prayer model:

Finger 1: Addressing our Father in Heaven

"Our Father which art in heaven ..."

Biblically, we are shown how Jesus always began his prayers by addressing his Father. In Matthew 6:9, he uses "Our Father in heaven." In his great intercessory prayer in John 17:1, and in his prayers on the cross in Luke 23:34, 46, Jesus addresses God as "Father." Mark 14:36 tells us Jesus addressed God as "Abba, Father," and in both Mark 15:34 and Matthew 27:46, Jesus used "My God, my God" to call upon his heavenly Father. In this first finger of prayer, Jesus teaches us to call upon the name of the Lord.

Finger 2: Offering praise to God

"Hallowed be thy name. Thy kingdom come. Thy will be done in earth, as it is in heaven."

Jesus always gave the praise, honor, and glory to God, and it is important to teach our children to praise his holy name in their prayer time! It is a way to show our humility, thankfulness, and love.

Finger 3: Laying needs before the Father

"Give us this day our daily bread. And forgive us our debts, as we forgive our debtors. And lead us not into temptation, but deliver us from evil . . ."

This is the heart of open prayer where healing, intercession, needs, and our need for forgiveness all come together in a powerful plea to the Father.

Finger 4: Praise and glory

"For thine is the kingdom, and the power, and the glory, forever."

This is a wonderful time to thank God for answered prayers and for the promises he has made and will keep in his faithfulness. This is the part where children can really say: "I love you, God."

Finger 5: Closing in his name

"I tell you the truth, my Father will give you whatever you ask in my name" (John 16:23, NIV).

Jesus teaches us that we are to ask in his name and our heavenly Father will hear and will answer. We close our prayers in the name of Jesus, amen!

These then are the five parts of the prayer model Jesus imparted to us through the Lord's Prayer; the perfect model given us by the Son to impart to

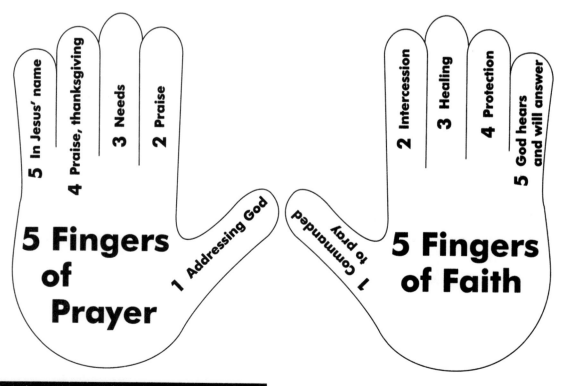

5 Fingers of Prayer

5 In Jesus' name
4 Praise, thanksgiving
3 Needs
2 Praise
1 Addressing God

5 Fingers of Faith

2 Intercession
3 Healing
4 Protection
5 God hears and will answer
1 Commanded to pray

our children. They are not hollow and devoid of praise or lacking in humility. Jesus' prayer specifically addresses his Father in heaven with needs and love echoing in every word. Jesus did not offer a rote prayer which is not really prayer at all. Instead, he composed a prayerful, praiseful, powerful love song to God and gave to us, by example, the perfect model of prayer.

Five Fingers of Faith

In addition to the above **5 Fingers of Prayer,** there are **5 Fingers of Faith** which our children must learn. These are biblical promises set forth by the Lord as a direct result of faithful prayer.

Finger 1: God commands us to pray.

It is important that our children realize prayer is not a parental invention to delay mealtime. It is what God has commanded of us. Jesus tells us to pray and not give up when we feel hopeless (Luke 18:1; 21:36). We are to pray if in trouble and to pray when needy (James 5:13; Matthew 7:7). In fact, God has commanded us to pray continually (1 Thessalonians 5:17)! "Pray in the spirit on all occasions with all kinds of prayers and requests" (Ephesians 6:18, NIV).

Finger 2: Intercession

With overpowering love spilling from each plea, Jesus' stirring prayer in chapter 17 of John illustrates perfectly how we are to reach out to the Father on behalf of others' needs. Jesus did not keep love to himself nor solve the disciples' burdens by himself; he lifted their needs to the Father through intercessory prayer. Our children need to learn this expression of love, lifting others up to God's throne through prayer.

"The prayer of a righteous man is powerful and effective" (James 5:16).

Finger 3: Healing

One of the most neglected promises of prayer is that of healing. In light of modern medicine and what we are told is better living through prescription chemicals, we have forgotten who the Great Physician is. He is God, our healer! The Healer of broken hearts, battered spirits, and crippled bodies. Our little ones must be taught that all power to heal lies in the hands of God. That by his divine will and in his time, we may be healed through faithful petitions in prayer.

"And the prayer offered in faith will make the sick person well . . . pray for each other so that you may be healed" (James 5:15,16).

Finger 4: Protection from evil

Troll dolls, peace amulets, crystals. Our children are being bombarded with symbolic charms to ward off bad luck, evil, and darkness. What a hey day Satan is having with our little ones. The very charms they wear to avoid these things are designed by Satan himself! This is warfare, and our children must be taught the truth: that the only way to deter Satan is through the power of faithful prayer. Jesus tells us to pray against temptation and sin (Matthew 26:41; Luke 22:40), and Ephesians 6:16 tells us to, above all, take up the shield of faith, our prayers!

"Watch and pray so that you will not fall into temptation" (Matthew 26:41).

Finger 5: God hears and answers prayer.

How many times has our faith wobbled as we've wondered if God really heard that prayer for a new job or a raise? God has promised he will hear each heart raised in prayer and will answer us. When God spoke to Zechariah, he promised that when we call upon his name, in prayer, he will hear and answer (Zechariah 13:9). Though our adult patience is supposed to exceed that of our child's, we both need to learn to wait upon the Lord in prayer with all faith that he will hear and answer each prayer we lift in Jesus' name.

"His ears are attentive to their prayer" (1 Peter 3:12).

Recap

Let's take a breather here and recap all that has been presented so far.

1. Prayer is our way of *fellowshiping* with God.
2. Powerful, effective, life-giving prayer must be *taught*.
3. Jesus provided us the perfect *prayer model*.
4. God gives us promises of *helping, healing, hearing, answering,* and *protection* through prayer.

Each of the prayer activities contained in the second half of this book is derived from the **5 Fingers of Prayer** model and based on at least one of the **5 Fingers of Faith.** As Christian parents and teachers, we must earnestly strive to go far beyond the rote and to offer our children the full teaching of prayer in all its intimacy, beauty, and power. It is a monumental task to be sure, but one exceedingly filled with abundant love—for you, your child, and the Father who holds your child so tenderly in his hands.

Step-By-Step

> "You're old enough to pray when you can put your hands together."
>
> **Michael, age 6**

In her book, "Children's Minds," Margaret Donaldson lists the following three key steps in the voyage from infancy through childhood: (1) making sense out of the world, (2) gaining control, and (3) using language. These three steps could be restated as: (1) reaction to the world, (2) development and control of emotion, and (3) communication skills. It is our accumulated reactions, emotions, and communications with others that shape and mold our earthly existence. And it is our collection of reactions, emotions, and communications between the Lord and our hearts that sweetly molds us into strong Christians, and prayer is inherent in each step.

This journey of development is sometimes slow and often frustrating; but if we want to understand and teach our children in the most effective way, we need to have a realistic grasp of their development. We need to know what they are and are not yet capable of and how they see and react to their world.

We could fill volumes describing and analyzing a multitude of developmental categories, such as physical, sexual, moral, social, and spatial; but in keeping with the relevancy of teaching prayer (and to avoid parental data overload), we will zero in on four specific areas of your child's development: verbal, emotional, reactionary, and spiritual. Each category will be briefly discussed in relation to the three age levels contained in the prayer activity section in the second half of this book: the two- to four-year-old, the five- and six-year-old and the seven- to ten-year-old.

Communication (verbal)

2- to 4-year-olds

Very young children learn spoken language rapidly, becoming fluent by age five in the language to which they have been exposed. A typical two- to early three-year-old has a spoken vocabulary (different from an understood vocabulary) of about 250 words which will increase dramatically over the next year and a half. By the time a child reaches his fourth birthday, his working vocabulary is close to 1500 words. Your little one is trying out sounds just for the pleasure of hearing how they sound as each one slides across his tongue. It doesn't matter that they make no sense to the adult ear, they are so much fun to say. This is the time when rhyming words, rhythmical sounding words, and alliteration (words all beginning with the same letter sound) are a delight to share with your little one.

Many small children in the third and fourth year begin using symbols to represent different words, so keep reading into the next age level for further explanation of this crucial development in your child's verbal communication skills.

5- to 6-year-olds

Representational thought is common in your young child of three to six years and is where symbols are used in place of people, objects, and actions. Symbolic activity is an important mode of expression for the youngster who is unable to express in words and abstractions those thoughts which are available to the older child and adult. In presenting prayer lessons to your three- to six-year-old, it is helpful to realize that prayer concepts (such as healing and intercession) may be made clearer if they are made representational; using an object to represent the concept as in a Band-Aid® for a reminder of healing or a telephone to explain how God hears us whenever we call. (See **Prayer Share Teddy Bear** and **Hot Line to Heaven** in activity section.) Again, even the concepts of healing, intercession, and omnipresence may be taught to your young child. It is only a matter of how to effectively present them in relation to where your child is developmentally!

7- to 10-year-olds

As language development continues and her working vocabulary increases with the advent of more complicated studies in school, your seven- to ten-year-old begins to move away from representational thought to concrete operations where she is able to mentally perform acts and ideas that she formerly carried out physically and through symbols. Now is the time to begin the shift toward more abstract prayer lessons where your child must reason, create, and express more independently and more through cognition than with her hands. (See **The Prayer Letter** in activity section.) Most barriers to communication are with a higher level of both spoken and understood vocabularies, and this increase in comprehension should be reflected in the lessons you offer on the power and fullness of prayer. However, and this is a BIG however, visual perception is very important in our culture where children receive a great deal of learning through video technology. As parents, we all know how tough it is to compete with video animation! If your child is given a choice between hearing a lesson and seeing/doing a lesson, he will no doubt opt for the visual choice.

Children do not learn by sight alone, but it is motivating and fun to sometimes offer them a prayer lesson that is visual and hands-on. Though some may think they are "too big for that stuff," they are still children at heart.

Emotional

According to Erik H. Erikson's developmental theory for childhood emotions, the two big emotional crises in a child's early life are: autonomy (self-sufficiency/trust) and initiative. In a secular sense, Erikson is theorizing "you are who you are as a result of self worth." As Christians, we know the *truth,* and how sweet it is, that we are who we are as a result of Jesus' love for us! It is important however to realize both basic trust and self-confidence are important to your child's development and equally relevant to the teaching of effective prayer. After all, it is the love of Jesus and the Father's faithfulness that we seek to teach our children through prayer, and that their trust and self-confidence come from him who loves them best.

2- to 4-year-olds

The sense of autonomy, or self-sufficiency/ trust, begins to blossom as your two- to three-year-old experiences the power of doing and deciding. Walking freely, manipulating toys, play tools, and puzzles all give your child a sensory security in his world and a chance to begin making some of his own decisions. "Shall I play with my truck or my airplane? I'll do it my way!" And if his way is not your way, conflicts may arise. Be patient, parents, for most often what appears as stubborn willfulness is actually developing assertiveness and is a strong predecessor to a healthy sense of self-respect in later years.

A toddler is keenly aware of other people's emotions; and though he may not comprehend why Mommy is crying, he certainly feels her hurt. Curiosity, mirth, anguish, and genuine sensitivity are plainly visible in a little one's eyes, and they are beginning to sense these feelings in others. This is the beauty of offering the seeds of intercession and the sweetness of praying for the ones your child so loves—and it is not too early.

Around the age of four, the sense of initiative captures center stage in your little one's emotional development. She is pushing vigorously into the world and exploring in an attempt to understand people, what they do, and what she herself is capable of. Grasping a slice of reality, your small daughter reaches for Daddy's briefcase and is "off to the office" in an exciting world of imagination set by example. Until this time, your wee ones merely imitated your words and actions, now you are setting examples of how and what to do. Praying through imitation and example are powerful ways to teach your young child (See **5 Fingers of**

> "But what if I don't do it right?"
>
> **Sarah, age 9**

Prayer in activity section), while giving him a sense of modeling and security. If you think back to nearly everything you have learned to do in your own life, it was no doubt learned through example or imitation set by either someone you respected or through observance of a particular skill, such as sewing.

Although a wide range of new emotions is flooding through your preschooler, it may be increasingly difficult for him to express feelings that are stemming from newness, limited language, shyness, and the fear of disapproval. Providing your little one with a safe way to express his emotions is a demonstration of your sensitivity. (See **Prayer Pal Puppet**.) Many, many children find it easier to talk through an inanimate object, such as a stuffed animal, pillow, or doll, and this is by no means unhealthy or abnormal; it merely allows any shyness or fear of judgment to fall away and helps your child to express himself more easily. Allow your little one this safe freedom of expression in his prayer time. I assure you, the loving Father will know your child is praying to him from the heart, expressing himself through his teddy bear, just as the Lord sometimes provides for us through other people.

5- to 6-year-olds

Finally . . . SCHOOL! School is the exciting educational and social key which opens the door to a huge, marvelous, and often frightening new world where Mom and Dad are no longer the sole focus of learning and authority in life. Suddenly, her teacher knows everything there is to know, is perfectly beautiful and just what your daughter wants to be when she grows up. From alphabets to reading first words to friendships made and lost in the wink of an eye, your beginning scholar is aflutter with daily "guess what I did in school" reports as the main course for dinnertime. So many concerns; so many questions. What a perfect opportunity to learn about leaving all things in God's hands through prayer; or how God truly hears and answers questions and concerns through prayer. (See **Prayer Hands** and **Picture Players**.)

Along with the advent of school days, comes a curious new malady that often upsets parents more than their child. The "nobody-likes-me" syndrome seems to creep silently onto playgrounds and into classrooms the world over. Your child is suddenly bewailing the fact that he doesn't have a friend in the whole world, let alone in his classroom! Be assured that in nearly all cases, this is not true; it is merely an exaggeration born of the struggles your little one is dealing with as he is exposed to a flood of new faces and peers. Over the years as a first grade teacher, I had to reassure many parents that little Melissa or Brad was not friendless; that a normal first grade friendship lasts strongly but a few weeks and should be given a gold medal if it survives a few months.

Normal, healthy kindergarten and first-graders play with many children during the school day, but this doesn't necessarily qualify them as friends in a child's definition. Think briefly about all of the people you know at work, church, your tennis league, and how even though you may eat with them or play golf with them, most are friendly acquaintances and not your best friends. You recognize that best friends are a precious gift from God and do not come along every day. Your child has not made this realization yet and needs you to help him know that not everyone we meet is going to be our close friend, but that does not mean we cannot be friendly with them. Now is the ideal time to focus prayer on Jesus as your child's true best friend and on caring for all people, as Jesus would want, through our prayers for them. (See **Prayer Share Teddy Bear**.)

7- to 10-year-olds

Self-esteem. How many of us have struggled, sometimes painfully, with our own self-doubts, shyness, and lack of confidence; allowing our fears about what others may think to rob us of all the special talents and gifts the Lord has given us? Remember that paper you dreaded to read before the whole third grade? Or the bit part in your fourth grade class play you were certain you would muddle? The biggest emotional concern our seven- to ten-year-olds face is lack of confidence, commonly expressed as terminal "I can'ts." (Isn't it wonderful we now know the dreaded "I can'ts" are indeed not terminal when we have Jesus in our life?)

Self-esteem is influenced greatly by what you tell your child about himself. Numerous studies have concluded that if you are a warm, supportive, and lovingly authoritative parent, your child will have a higher, more secure concept of himself. Add to this the single most important element from which your child should gain his self-concept—the Father—and you will be well on the way on the Christian path of nurturing your child's self-esteem to be its best. (See **Can Do Prayers**.)

A great concern of seven- to ten-year-olds when it comes to prayer (indeed, of most ages even well into adulthood!), is the concern they will do it wrong. This is the number one reason children have given for not praying when I have asked them if they would like to pray aloud for our children's Bible group. And this reason has held true for many children from homes where prayer is common with their parents. Many parents think they are praying with their children when actually they are praying for their children. It is easier to handle this reluctance at praying aloud by praying for them, but you must realize what the reluctance stems from and teach beyond it.

I have compiled a list of the top five prayer concerns of this age group and I believe they are very representative of adult concerns as well.

1. How do I pray?
2. Should I sit or kneel or stand?
3. Should I use any special words when I pray?
4. Do I fold my hands or lift my hands?
5. Should I pray silently or is it okay to pray out loud?

Any of these concerns, when not addressed, may build walls to hinder your child from giving to God what he so deeply desires—your child's heart in prayer. The fear of how to give may smother that which we so greatly seek to offer. When you teach your child about God's unconditional, all accepting love, assure him that God does not care whether he sits or kneels or prays silently or sings a prayer; the Father just wants to hear from the one he so greatly loves . . . YOU! And as your child begins to gain more confidence through your teaching and the prayer activities offered here, you will notice a willingness to offer up prayer more openly and to share prayer and praise aloud. (See **The Prayer Letter** and **Present Prayers**.)

Reactionary

Reactionary development could best be described as the way in which a child acts and reacts to his world; how he strives to make sense out of his environment and the people around him. How a child reacts to and manipulates his environment has great impact on how he will learn prayer concepts. For this reason, reaction is the twin sister to the learning styles that will be discussed in the following chapter.

2- to 4-year-olds

Sensory. No other word comes close to the way in which a little one reacts to his world. Every object, living or inanimate, is fair game for a taste, touch, or sniff. Grapes travel to ears, toy trucks to the tongue and oatmeal turns to marvelous finger paint before the often distraught eyes of parents.

Tactile, sensory exploration is the forerunner to communication and expression. How often has your little one reached for a pot on the stove and you've said, "Hot!" He puts the word hot with the feeling of great warmth and begins to physically understand the abstract concept of heat. Through the touch of sand, a child understands grittiness; through the taste of a lemon, he communicates sour.

Provide tactile ways for your child to "feel" his way around his world and re-

member, next time he reaches for that curious glass rooster on grandmother's shelf, that physical touch is the first step to communication. How did your little one begin to understand trust, love and acceptance? Through the touch of your gentle hands!

5- to 6-year-olds

Where the two- to four-year-old may be thought of as a discoverer, your five- to six-year-old is more the explorer. Still very much a tactile learner, your child is learning how to skillfully act on his environment; to change it, alter it, or erase it. Instead of laying blocks in a row as she did a few years earlier, your six-year-old daughter now piles them into an entire castle. She knows a block is used in building, but now she begins to explore concepts, such as height, balance, shape, and how the blocks work with and against each other.

Kindergarten and first-graders are learning to react with less reflex and more thought. Storing up the way things work physically, your child is able to begin drawing abstract conclusions before witnessing the actual event. He sees 5 apples, imagines 2 rolling away, and concludes that 3 are left to eat. Subtraction abstraction! It is just such abstract reasoning that will help your child move into deeper faith with the Lord through prayer. After all, faith is the heart abstractly knowing what the eyes cannot physically see.

7- to 10-year-olds

The focus on tactile reactions begins to wane as your child's vocabulary and life experiences grow. The drive to touch everything on the gift shop shelf has lessened as your child understands physical boundaries by this age and is able to contain his sense of curiosity.

Your seven- to ten-year-old is learning to react to the world in a mental and emotional way, forming opinions, conclusions, and feelings in response to his environment and the people around him. A sense of logical cause and effect has begun to emerge and, along with this sense, the seeds of morality and right and wrong. Your child is now able to begin comprehending and nurturing reverential fear of the Lord; that disobedience and punishment go together as closely as obedience and blessings; that because of our many sins, Jesus died to bring us glorious salvation and fellowship with our Father in Heaven.

Spiritual

Spiritual development is rarely touched by any scholar or student of human development. It does not lend itself to any earthly rod of measurement; no test will register a score; no assessment, a standard of achievement. Spirituality is strictly between the Father and each of us alone. Yet though we cannot measure our development, there is something we can do. We can pray for continual growth in learning God's Word, in living in the center of God's will, of discerning his wisdom, and of seeking his face. As parents, and as grateful stewards of his beloved children, it is our godly duty to nurture our children's growth in Christian education; in prayer!

We cannot measure spiritual readiness

as we can verbal usage, but as a parent and Christian educator, I can assure you of this: virtually any biblical lesson may be taught at any age level. It is never a question of what can be taught at an age, but rather how to teach it. Certainly your young child will not comprehend a given lesson as an adult would, but he will understand it in the context of his own age. If you read a Scripture verse today, you will understand its meaning in the context of your present moment. Yet have you ever read a verse over at a later time and said, "WOW! I never saw that before?" This is the wondrous beauty of God's Word; it is always new, always relevant, always growing. And the same is true for a child. What you teach your child today will be built upon, as God directs, over his entire lifetime.

As adults, we must pray against complacency and stagnation in our relationship with God, that we will never cease to discover more meaning in each verse we study. If we see today only that which we saw yesterday, something is very wrong. May we reach and teach our children to continually seek God's refreshment and newness in their daily prayers and praise.

With such a deluge of developments to digest, it may be helpful to compile them into a flow chart, remembering that each new development is but an extension of one established at an earlier age. The goal in understanding your child's development and capabilities is to realize he is truly a delightful and unique creation and will develop, at God's direction and timing, into God's cherished servant and prayer warrior.

> "My spirit is my heart God gives me."
>
> **Aaron, age 7**

AGE	VERBAL	EMOTIONAL	REACTIONARY	LEARNING STYLES
2 **to** **4**	Average vocabulary of 1000 words Imitates sounds Enjoys rhyming words Learning beginning letter sounds	Egocentric Shy around strangers Imitates in play; pretends Confident; easily motivated Learning autonomy	Sensory Reacts physically to world and other people Reacts out of reflex not thought	See chapter 3 Concrete; hands on Visual stimulus Imitation and example Songs and rhymes
5 **to** **6**	Average vocabulary of about 2500 words Beginning to read and write Expresses feelings openly Representational thought	Teacher as new authority figure Worries about friends/peers Sensitive to others' feelings and needs Wants to please	Tactile Explores more abstract concepts Reacts with more thought and less reflex	Concrete; hands on Visual Example Beginning conceptual Creative
7 **to** **10**	Good written communication Able to put abstract ideas and feelings into words Concrete operations instead of representational thought	Peer pressures high, wants to fit in More closed in sharing feelings Self-doubts begin to emerge More independent	Less need for the sensory, but still enjoyed Quite good at abstract thinking and reasoning Wants to know "why"	Conceptual, but still enjoys concrete Creative Handles a variety of learning styles Easily bored if repetitious

ABC—123

During my years as an elementary schoolteacher, there were times when I would suggest that parents give extra help to tutor a little one over a math or reading hump. Often came the same reply, "But, Susan, I am not a teacher; I don't know how to teach my kids!" But I will assure you, as I did them; you are already a teacher. I have never met a person who is not a teacher. We all have a lesson to learn and a lesson to teach, because this is God's way of helping us to be humble and to rely on each other for growth. It is not that you do not know how to teach, you just need to know how to present your lesson effectively.

This chapter is devoted to giving you the educational strategies you need to implement effective lessons in prayer.

> "Where did God learn to make the world? What school did he go to to learn all that?"
>
> **Amy, age 4**

You already have a good idea of where your child is in relation to his verbal and emotional development and what is reasonable for him to comprehend at his age. It is here we shall put this knowledge to use and hone the tools to carve powerful lessons in prayer upon your child's heart and mind.

Educational strategies have their foundations in the various styles of learning, which include: verbal, visual, written, auditory, concrete, and conceptual. With many years of schooling behind us, we know which method was easiest for us. I learned most quickly with hands-on projects and reinforced them with written reports. Had I been forced into one mode of learning, such as lectures and note-taking, I would surely have seen different grades on my report cards. What a blessing that there are so many individual ways for individual people to learn.

Styles of Learning

In this chapter, we will take a look at three main learning styles: concrete, visual, and conceptual. Within the framework of these three styles, geared to their age appropriateness, you are bound to discover genuine excitement in teaching your child to pray. Let us turn our attention to the first learning style we will cover: CONCRETE learning.

Concrete

Concrete learning is just what its name implies: solid, strong, touchable. Commonly referred to as "hands-on" learning in classroom lingo, concrete learning is a physical way to teach a lesson. I could tell you about an apple by describing its fiery red skin, fruity fragrance, and juicy flesh; but if you had never seen an apple before, it would mean little. To truly understand what an apple is all about, you would have to experience its color, odor, and taste by holding it and feeling it and biting deeply into its crisp coolness. Only then would you know what an apple is. This is concrete learning, allowing the senses to understand that which words do not provide.

Hands-on learning is perfectly suited to the very young child who reacts to his world in a tactile way. Toy manufacturers know this well. Puzzles, games, puppets, finger rhymes, and hand held objects (which represent a concept or idea) are good vehicles for getting prayer objectives across to your young child in a fun, motivating way. It is less like work and more like fun with hands-on lessons that provide powerful teaching in a painless format.

Many of the prayer lessons/activities in the second half of this book are good examples of the concrete learning style, including: **Hot Line to Heaven** for the two- to four-year-old, **Prayer Share Teddy Bear** for the five- and six-year-old and the **Prayer Warrior** for older children. Make use of hands-on learning whenever possible and remember that prayer is both a hands-on and hearts-on gift to God.

Visual

Visual learning goes (pardon the pun) hand in hand with hands-on learning. What concrete objects do for the hands, visual pictures do for the eyes. Imagine being blind from birth and having your friend try to define the concept of: RED. Pretty tough challenge when you think about it. But if you were to suddenly gain your sight and could see the color of a fire engine, you would finally understand this thing called red.

A picture paints a thousand words, but to a young child, these words mean little; it's the picture that counts. In fact, the picture teaches the lesson. And because of a limited vocabulary, it is far easier for little ones to learn in a visual mode as evidenced by the tremendous number of picture books for children that are available. Visual learning not only delights the eye and stimulates the imagination, it empowers understanding.

Jesus knew well the power of both concrete and visual learning. He used both in many of the lessons he taught. Creating pictures of familiar objects, Jesus described himself as the living *Vine* (John 15:1), the *Bread* of life (John 6:35) and the *Gate* (John 10:7). These were objects the crowds knew and could relate to; objects the crowds could understand. If Jesus had only said, "You need me greatly," it would not have had the impact that bread of life had. The people knew that bread was life to them; and they were able to begin to comprehend that Jesus, like bread, was life to them. Take this heavenly cue from Jesus' lessons and offer your children concrete, visual learning for prayers.

Conceptual

Conceptual learning involves direct mental imaging; it is a higher learning style than either concrete or visual and becomes more functional as a child increases both his vocabulary and his personal experience. It may help to imagine you are standing on a grassy riverbank. Before you is running a wide creek. On the other side is a flower you wish to pick. If you are small and unable to leap the creek without help, you may need a concrete stepping stone to help you get to the flower. But in the event you are older, you will be able to make the leap without concrete help. Conceptual learning, then, is making the leap to a concept or idea without the help of a physical object.

Good techniques for conceptual learning include asking stimulating questions beginning with: "What do you think would happen if . . ." or "How do you feel when . . ." or "Why do you suppose . . ." Using analogies to get a point across is a conceptual strategy as well as reading Scripture and drawing conclusions that lead into your lesson.

As adults, we use conceptual learning daily to form opinions and thoughts as we watch the news, read a book, or listen to the boss. We speak in conceptual terms almost exclusively. But the biggest mistake we make when attempting to teach our young children is that we take for granted they are able to comprehend by these same adult conceptual means, and our best intentions sail right over their small heads. Watch for clues that tell you she may not be grasping the goal of your lesson fully. Wandering eyes and silent nods of the head often indicate ideas are going past the heart and not into it. If this is the case, try using a more concrete approach before returning to the conceptual.

Teaching prayer with conceptual methods is a valuable strategy for stimulating your older child to think about what Jesus has truly given us through the power of faithful prayer; where concrete learning is hands-on, conceptual learning is hearts-on.

In addition to the three key learning styles, it is vital to grasp the importance of learning through *imitation* and *example* and how to retain a lesson once it has been mastered.

Though mentioned in Chapter 2, imitation and example are worthy of another plug in our discussion of learning styles and teaching strategies. Both imitation and example are teaching methods that provide your child with security in trying out a new skill or concept. Effective in teaching prayer, imitation allows your little one to parrot back certain prayer phrases that the parent/teacher presents, and when the phrases are used with accompanying hand gestures (visual learning), this is a strong method for teaching a child to pray according to Jesus' prayer model. (See **Echo Prayers** for the 5- to 6-year-olds and **Prayer Pal Puppet** for 2- to 4-year-olds.)

Example is a close cousin of imitation, but example, unlike imitation, does not mirror the words or actions; it offers a sample to cling to before the child can take the independent step of freely creating his own prayer. (See **Prayer Letter** in the 7- to 10-year-old section.)

Three R's of Retention

As a former student, you are familiar with the 3 R's of schooling, but as a teacher, you need to be aware of the 3 R's of RETENTION: *Reteaching, Reinforcement,* and *Reward.* These three are the key ingredients to locking what has been learned into heart and mind and retaining those precious prayer lessons. Merely presenting a concept once will not ensure it has been understood or will be remembered in a few days, let alone a lifetime! You must seek to strengthen and build your child's retention muscle after you have presented a lesson. Here are the 3 R's of Retention:

1. *Reteaching* is going back over a concept that your child has not fully grasped. Try presenting your prayer lesson a day or two later, perhaps in a more concrete or visual way. After you feel the concept has been learned, proceed with reinforcement.

2. *Reinforcement* is the act of reviewing what has been learned. Without regular reinforcement, learning tends to fade. Keep prayer concepts bright and strong by regular review.

3. *Reward* is a lesson's "dessert," enriching what has been learned in a fun, motivating way. A game or shared activity, done solely for the joy of doing, is a great reward for hard work.

By putting the 3 R's of retention to regular use, your child is building and strengthening his prayer muscle, and you are helping to provide insurance that the power packed lessons in prayer you are teaching will be locked in your child's heart and mind for a lifetime.

Recap

Time for another brief recap of learning styles and approaches to teaching your child prayer (and anything else!):

* Learning styles are varied and must be age appropriate to be effective teacher tools.
* There are three main learning styles in young children: *concrete, visual,* and *conceptual.*
* *Concrete* and *visual* styles are best suited to small children. (Although the older child still desires some hands-on activities and may need the extra boost that concrete/visual learning provides.)

* *Conceptual* learning is geared for the older child, but watch to make sure he is understanding the lesson.
* *Imitation* and *example* provide secure models for learning.
* The 3 R's of *Retention* strengthen prayer concepts for memory.

Feeling ready to tackle the tasks of teaching? You now have the background, the teaching tools, the pupil, and the most powerful principal of all to support you in your lessons: the Lord!

The second half of this book is full of age appropriate, child tested, Bible-based prayer lessons for you to offer your children. Each one is based on a biblical concept (**Fingers of Faith**) and supported by the model of prayer Jesus gave us so long ago (**Fingers of Prayer**).

It is my own fervent prayer that our precious children become the powerful prayer warriors the Lord desires them to be. There is power in the prayers of a child: to lift broken hearts, to mend battle scarred families, to melt away fear and strike down loneliness, and to praise God with joy and laughter. For armed with teddy bears, sneakers, and prayers to their heavenly Father, our little ones shall be the tiny warriors of God.

"Though her voice is small and mild, All Heaven stills for the prayers of a child!"

ACTIVITY SECTION

Tips for Using the Activity Section

1. The prayer activities and lessons included in the following pages are not to be used only one time. Rotate them in order to offer your child variety and good reinforcement of the prayer concepts you teach. Prayer should not be the same each time you approach the throne of God because needs and emotions change daily and prayer times should also be new and fresh.

2. Keep the prayer aids and helps you make in a special box. This teaches the idea that some things are very special and are set aside just for God. Keep your prayer box in a special place and pull out the items when you desire to use them. They will be ready to teach for years to come and the box will make a precious Christian keepsake to pass along to your tiny grandchildren.

3. Check other age groups in the activity section for a prayer help or lesson you can adapt to your child's needs. If your child is very small, remember that these activities build on each other throughout the three age groups presented, so the book will grow along with your child. If your child is a little older, please check the younger age levels for ideas to adapt. The lessons presented at the earlier ages are vital for older children to learn as well.

4. The prayer reinforcement charts at the end of each age section are reproducible. Photocopy them and rotate to keep the daily prayer momentum rolling in a fun way. Again, check other age sections for extra charts you may wish to use.

Praying With Your 2-4 Year Old

Characteristics

What is more exciting, more miraculous, and more delightful than a tiny caterpillar emerging from his cocoon as a graceful butterfly? The answer to this riddle is easy for parents of toddlers. It is the glorious transformation of a tiny two-year-old as he blossoms into a fabulous four-year-old! At no other time in your child's life will energetic learning, growth, and change come together to create such a power packed metamorphosis. Your cuddly "caterpillar" will, in just three short years, blossom into a beautiful butterfly ready to fly off to school.

The packaging of such dynamic human energy in this tiny bundle of precious precociousness is truly God's sweetest of miracles. Fueled by insatiable curiosity, your little one's first words following "Da Da" and "Ma Ma" may just be "Whasszat?" (Translation: What is that?) Rushing headlong from one object or idea to the next, you may wonder where she gets all that energy. Just tell yourself her energy comes from you and that is why you are always running low!

Create times to slow your small steam engine down a bit. A warm cuddle session and a colorful Bible picture book will create a cozy mood for quietly feeding your little one's curiosity with God's presence in picture. Ask him to locate objects, such as the rainbow or the ark, or people, such as Mary or Moses or Jesus.

With the wondrous achievement of potty training comes a newfound sense of autonomy and self-confidence. This is certainly the most contented time of self-confidence we ever have in life. Everything is possible to a toddler! Everything about him shouts "I can!" and if there is frustration, it is only perceived as a nuisance, not a wall. If someone playfully tells a child with a shovel that he could dig to China, the little one begins throwing dirt every which way! Ahh, for the faith of a child.

Communication skills in the two- to four-year-old are growing by leaps and bounds; and if her vocabulary is not that of an adult as yet, she is an accomplished master of total body language. From the mischievous glint in her eye as your little one reaches for Miss Kitty's whiskers to the stomping foot when a gumball is not on the shopping list, your toddler has a wide and growing range of language skills.

This is an ideal time to begin work on beginning letter sounds and what better book can you use than *the Book*? Taking a cue from the bright illustrations in his Bible picture book, target one beginning letter sound per week (steering clear of vowels) and ask your child to find pictures beginning with that letter. Find the "R-rrrrr rainbow," the "R-rrrr river," etc. Have your little one rrrr-repeat the sound and the word before going to the next picture. Just a word here about the types of children's Bibles and Bible related books that are appropriate for this age level. For 2-, 3- and 4-year-olds, Bible picture books offer a wealth of stimulating learning, provided the pictures are colorful and simple. Few, if any, words are needed in books for very young children as they learn almost exclusively in a visual way.

Bible storybooks are a delight for the older 3- and 4-year-old but be sure they are well illustrated. Toddlers have a difficult time envisioning what words describe and need pictures to help them have a clearer and fuller understanding of each story.

It is important to choose a children's Bible that does not limit or water down God's Word. Please think before purchasing a child's Bible that contains only the New Testament or one which contains no Scripture but just flowery descriptions of Scripture. You cannot be nourished on descriptions of food; it must be eaten if you are to grow strong, and so it is with God's Word!

Suggested Prayer Times

Three short prayer times of no longer than 5 minutes each are realistic for your very young child. If your little one tires quickly, be flexible. Never force your tiny one into prayer or prolong prayer time past his attention span. Prayer is not the object of a power play! Be patient and flexible in allowing your little one to set the pace for a while. Remember, you are only in the beginning stages of establishing an attitude of prayer in your little one's heart. Prayer should be peaceful, enjoyable, warm, and daily, not forced.

Main Idea to Be Presented

"GOD LOVES YOU!" This is the most important foundation you can impart to your tiny child—that God loves him or her ALWAYS, NO MATTER WHAT, NO MATTER WHEN, NO MATTER

WHERE! He will always be with us, loving us and protecting us. Help him to see God's love every day by noticing the beauty in the world around your child and saying, "Oh, look at the sunrise! God certainly loves us to have created such beauty!" or, "I'm sorry you skinned your knee. God feels bad, too, because he loves you so much! He will help your knee to heal because he cares for you and wants you well." There are countless ways to praise God and his great love all through your day.

Your young child will be able to memorize a Scripture verse to show him of God's great love. During a prayer-share time, read 1 John 4:19 aloud and let your child repeat it back to you. Ask him often during the next few days to repeat the verse, and soon he will be singing it aloud. John 3:16 should be a fun challenge for your older 3- or 4-year-old. (See **God Loves You** activity.)

One-Step-Further Concept

Prayer allows us to talk with God through Jesus, the Son. And many small children, though they have been exposed to the name of Jesus, still have only a vague idea of who he really is. It may help to draw a picture of your family and have your child identify the members. Then draw a picture of God and Jesus (perhaps a cloud with GOD written inside and Jesus below). Have your child circle the father in the family picture and then circle God, the Father, in the other picture. Then allow him to circle the child in the family picture and Jesus in the other. Tell him that Jesus is the only child of God, the Father.

On your drawing of the holy family, draw your child next to Jesus and say, "We can talk to God in our prayers if we use Jesus' name. When we talk to God in the name of Jesus, our prayers are heard by God." (*Draw an arrow from your child to Jesus and from Jesus to God.*)

This should help you to teach the concept of praying in the name of Jesus. Let your child color the picture of the holy family and then hang it in his room to enjoy.

Now turn the page to find fun activities for teaching your 2- to 4-year-old to pray.

5 Fingers of Prayer

Very small children enjoy finger rhyme songs, and this "5 Fingers of Prayer" song combines the motivation of a finger rhyme song with the concept of the prayer model Jesus gave to us. Based on the **5 Fingers of Prayer** (*See Chapter 1*), this song uses that prayer pattern in an echo style presentation (*imitation*).

(Note: Though you only need your five fingers to do this prayer song for your little one, you could also use a glove with various pictures attached to the fingertips to illustrate the song. The suggested pictures are placed to the right of the ECHO part.)

Sung to the tune of: "Where Is Thumbkin?"

PARENT.............................ECHO (child)   **Finger motions**

HOLY FATHER ....holy Father,
I LOVE YOU ....I love you.
YOU'RE WITH ME EVERY DAY,
WHEN I COME TO PRAY,
IN HIS NAME ....in his name.

HOLY FATHER ....holy Father,
YOU ARE KING ....you are king
YOU'RE WITH ME EVERY DAY,
WHEN I COME TO PRAY,
IN HIS NAME ....in his name.

HOLY FATHER ....holy Father,
I NEED YOU ....I need you.
YOU'RE WITH ME EVERY DAY,
WHEN I COME TO PRAY,
IN HIS NAME ....in his name.

HOLY FATHER ....holy Father,
I GIVE YOU THANKS ....I give you thanks
YOU'RE WITH ME EVERY DAY,
WHEN I COME TO PRAY,
IN HIS NAME ....in his name.

HOLY FATHER ....holy Father,
STAY BY ME........................stay by me
YOU'RE WITH ME EVERY DAY,
WHEN I COME TO PRAY,
IN HIS NAME ....in his name.

"God Loves You" POSTER

You will need: scissors, markers (or crayons), glue

This is a page for you and your little one to do together. It is meant to reinforce the idea that God loves YOU! Cut off the top of this page on the lines, and then cut off the bottom row of small pictures. Cut the pictures apart and ask your little one to identify each. (*The heart stands for the word LOVE.*)

Glue each picture in the correct box, matching shapes on the upper right corner of the small picture to the one in the center of the box. When you are finished, have your child "read" the two verses he has made. (*Help him with the words, of course.*) Now let him color his mini poster and hang it up in his room to read over and over again. In your prayer-share time, thank God for his great love.

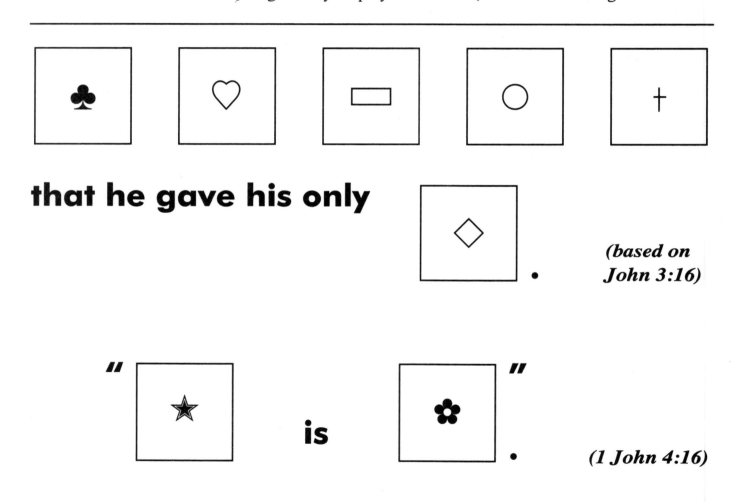

that he gave his only

(based on John 3:16)

is

(1 John 4:16)

Spread Apart Heart

You will need: red poster board (white will work), 1 brass brad, scissors, markers, tacky or clear tape, small squares of white paper, small photo of your child (if desired)

This prayer lesson is presented in a visual, hands-on way. It teaches that prayer is our way of telling God what is inside our hearts, what we are feeling, when we are hurt or sick or thankful or happy, what we are afraid of, and how much we love our Father!

Make the Spread Apart Heart by using the pattern below and cutting out 2 red hearts. Cut one heart in half and attach the brad through all 3 pieces at the point. (*NOTE: You will have to slightly overlap the two halves at the tip. See diagram #1.*) Your heart should now spread apart.

#1 whole heart — brad

#2 Dane's Heart (whole heart is behind two halves) — brad

Now, write your child's name on half of the front heart piece. Glue her photo on the other side. (*See diagram #2*).

Suggestion for use:

Tell your little one that God loves her very much and wants to know what she is feeling in her heart. Is she happy or sad? Is she afraid or feeling sick? Is there someone she thinks of often that may need God's help? Choose one or two of her responses and draw them on small white squares of paper. Spread open the heart and gently tack or tape them to the whole heart. Now close the heart front.

As you and your child "prayer share," allow her to open up her heart to the Father and tell him what is (literally) in her heart. The pictures will help your little one to better verbalize her emotions.

cut 2

Fingertip Prayers

You will need: 1 old glove, 1 foot of Velcro, markers, scissors, poster board, glue (*Note: Use the small pictures on the next page on the glove's fingertips.*)

Fingertip Prayers are sweet, motivating prayers that are right at the tips of your fingers! Use a glove with Velcro on the fingertips. The small picture pieces from the next page can be attached to its fingertips. Then the glove can be used to give your prayer time added color, fun, and learning. The first rhyme below uses the five hearts on the bottom of the next page to help you begin to establish a pattern for effective, full prayer based on the Lord's Prayer prayer model. (*See Chapter 1.*)

To make Velcro glove and picture pieces:
Attach small strips of Velcro (rough side) to the inside fingertips of a glove. Color the picture pieces on the next page and glue the whole page to a piece of poster board. (*Cover in clear contact paper if desired.*) Cut out pictures and attach Velcro (smoother side) strips to backs of pieces. Picture pieces should now stick to the fingertips of the glove. (*Use as directed with each Fingertip Prayer rhyme.*)

palm

5 Little Prayers

1. This little prayer says: "I LOVE YOU!"

2. This little prayer says: "YOU'RE GOD!"

3. This little prayer says: "I NEED YOU!"

4. This little prayer says: "YOU'RE MY FRIEND!"

5. This little prayer says: "IN JESUS' NAME, AMEN!"

1

2 GOD

3

4

5

Thank You, God

Thank you, God, for your great love

For earth below and skies above;

And when I'm scared and feeling blue,

May I give my fears to YOU?

In Jesus' name, amen.

JESUS

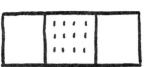

Fingertip Prayer PATTERNS

and extra prayer pictures to help express feelings

Set A   Use these pictures as your child desires. They may help him to more easily express his feelings, needs, prayers for others, etc. You may wish to tell him what each picture represents in prayer. After a short time, he will catch on!

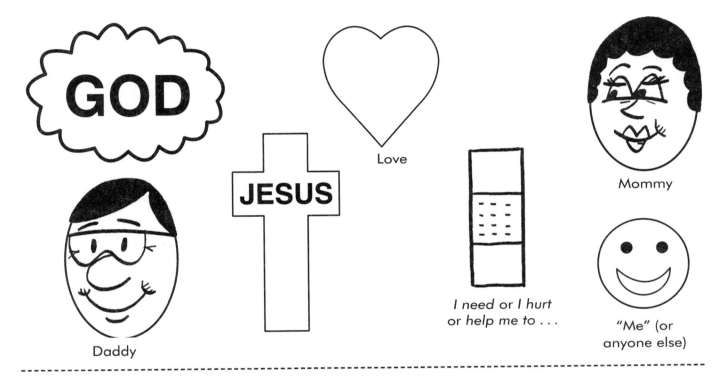

GOD

Love

Mommy

JESUS

I need or *I hurt*
or *help me to* . . .

"Me" (or
anyone else)

Daddy

Set B   Use this set of hearts with the **Fingertip Prayer**: "5 Little Pray-ers"

Prayer Pal Puppet

You will need: 1 (or 2) white lunch sacks, scissors, colored construction paper, glue, markers, yarn (if desired for hair), patterns on next page

It is sometimes difficult for very young children to express feelings, and a puppet is often a "safe" way for little ones to verbalize. This Prayer Pal does just that, plus it gives valuable reinforcement of Jesus' prayer model at the same time! Beginning at the lips, we address the Father; the heart is a reminder to praise him with love; the puppet's right hand reminds your child to ask God's help in his life while the left hand is for asking help for others' needs or hurts. The Prayer Pal ends with the reminder that we always pray in the name of Jesus.

Suggestions for use:

Your child is in a stage that's filled with learning through imitation and example. The first time you present Prayer Pal Puppet, it would be a good idea if you "go first." As you offer a simple prayer, follow the pieces on your prayer pal in order, using each as a guide for your prayer. (*Order: mouth, heart, hands, Jesus*) Point to each piece as you pray that section; this will help establish the pattern for effective prayer that Jesus gave to us in his prayer model with the Lord's Prayer. (*See Chapter 1.*)

Now it's your child's "turn." Allow him to make up his own prayer, but help guide him by pointing to each piece and leading him to pray about each one. After a few prayer times, your little one will catch on and will soon need no Prayer Pal to help him remember to praise and pray more fully. What a grand start to an intimate life of prayer with our heavenly Father.

Pattern pieces for
Prayer Pal Puppet

Dear heavenly Father

I Love you

- Color
- Cut out pieces
- Glue to sack

I also pray for

Please help me to

IN JESUS' NAME, AMEN

Hot Line to Heaven

You will need: 1 piece of white poster board, scissors, crayons or markers, glue, 1 foot of curling ribbon, glitter (optional)
(*If you have an old, real or play telephone, this is very effective.*)

This prayer lesson teaches about God's promise of always being "on call" for us when we pray to him—ANY time, ANY place, for ANYthing we need! Since small children understand and learn better through visual and concrete methods, the **Hot Line to Heaven** is a hands-on way to introduce your child to the security of knowing he is able to "call" on the name of the Lord ANY time in prayer. The telephone is a familiar object to even small ones and this helps to make this concept clearer.

Use the patterns on the next page to construct your **Hot Line to Heaven.** (*See diagram below for how finished activity should appear.*) As you work together, explain to your child that we cannot really call God on a telephone, but we have a much FASTER, much BETTER way to call him— through PRAYER and in the name of JESUS!

OUR HEAVENLY FATHER

Suggestions for use:

Gently attach the heavenly cloud to a wall, a chair or dresser, or even the ceiling for some real excitement! (*You will have to add an "extension ribbon" for this.*) Ask your child to think about the things he might say to God in his prayers. Then allow your little one to "call" upon the name of the Lord and pray using his **Hot Line to Heaven.** (*Read Jeremiah 33:3 aloud to your child.*)

For older 3's and 4-year-olds who are beginning to learn their letters, this is a fun time to let them touch-tone dial the letters J-E-S-U-S, for it is through HIS name that we pray. Remind them that we always pray in the name of Jesus; that prayer allows us to talk to God through his Son.

On reverse side, write,
"Hot Line to Heaven"
(Be sure to brightly
color your phone!)

J
E
S
U
S

"Call to me and I will answer you!" Jeremiah 33:3

OUR HEAVENLY FATHER

Optional:
Glue glitter on edges

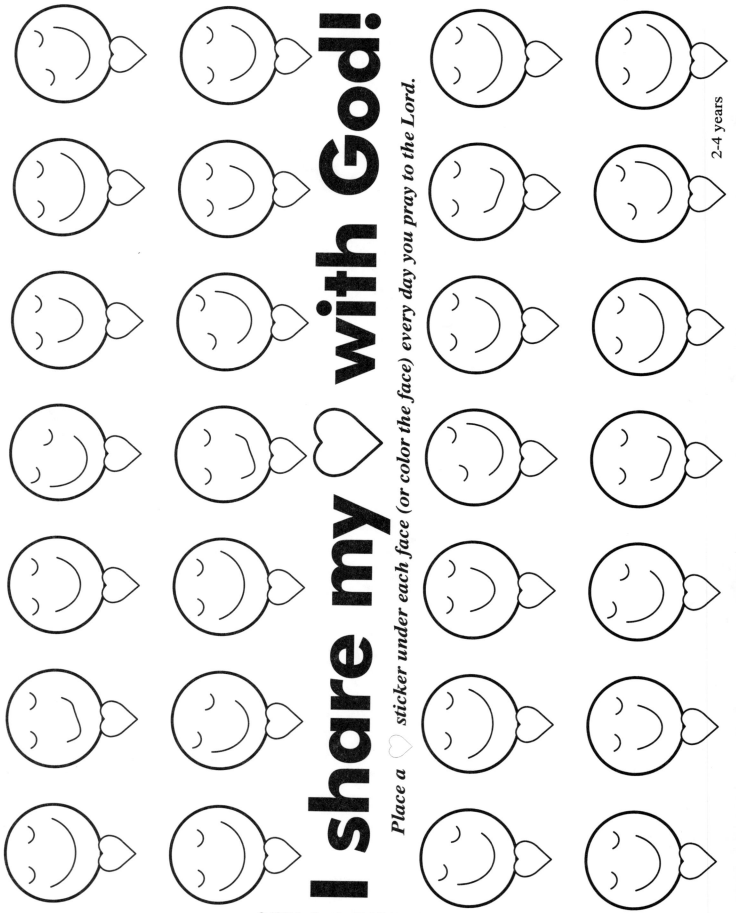

I share my ♡ with God!

Place a ♡ sticker under each face (or color the face) every day you pray to the Lord.

2-4 years

I am a prayerful . . .

lamb of God!

Glue a cotton ball on a circle each day you pray.

2-4 years

Praying With Your 5-6 Year Old

Characteristics

Open, honest, eager to learn, and even more eager to please, the five- or six-year-old is a bubbling fountain of nonstop energy! Suddenly, the baby has disappeared and a new, more confident little one is emerging into full, radiant blossom, complete with a newly developing autonomy. School, new friends, and the most marvelous "invention" called a TEACHER have entered the five- or six-year-old's life!

No longer totally reliant upon his parents for fulfilling needs and wants, the young beginning scholar is embarking on a voyage of newfound trust in other figures of authority. It seems as if overnight the parent no longer knows things of importance; and this is echoed in statements, such as "That's not what we learned in school today!" or "But Mrs. Sanders said . . ." Parents with fragile egos may wince at these words or feel a twinge of sadness to know their child's learning no longer revolves solely around them. But rejoice, for this is how the Lord has planned the circles of love and trust to flow and grow.

As the five- or six-year-old widens his arena of trust, he begins to understand and experience the world around him in a new, often shaky, sometimes scary, but always beautiful light! If a child did not grow and discover the wealth of life and learning around him, how would he ever be able to serve Jesus and love others as he has been commanded? Take

> "Jesus is my friend. I always talk to my friends."
>
> Sarah B.

heart and be glad for this new-found independence, for it, too, is a gift of God.

If new freedom and independence is a novel treat for the five- to six-year-old child, his increased attention span is a wonderful novelty for the parent. The perpetual motion of the three- and four-year-old has been tempered into a slightly slower speed, measured in rounds per minute instead of rounds per millisecond! Longer attention spans for the five- and six-year-old may mean slower mealtimes, longer bedtime stories, and more time for prayer; though certainly every moment counts.

With the beginning of school, arrives the ALPHABET and beginning reading skills. Five- and six-year-olds may begin to recognize high frequency words, and this is a good time to introduce them to the written words: *Jesus, God, amen, Lord,* etc. Short words with distinct sounds will be easy for them to recognize; and there is nothing more beautiful than the proud smile of confidence and accomplishment on the face of a beginning reader!

The focus of the five- and six-year-old is still greatly upon SELF, but that focus is beginning to widen into a circle that includes parents, siblings, and teachers. Use this growing awareness to begin encouraging your child to pray for the needs of others. A little one is capable of the first seeds of intercessory prayer, and this need to care and love through prayer should be gently nurtured. If the family has a pet, it is typically prayed over by a small child; and some parents wonder if this is proper or biblical. Rejoice in the

> *"An' I wonder if he sees me smile when I pray or laugh."*
>
> Jeremy A.

tender heart of your child who is able to feel love for a multitude. Love, to a little one, is pure, simple, and unconditional, whether it's for a person or animal or any other of the Lord's bountiful and beautiful creations. Isn't this purity the essence of love and caring? Allow your child to pray what is in his heart, and let God be the judge of his prayers.

Suggested Prayer Times

As the five-year-old's attention span lengthens into the even longer span of the six-year-old, prayer times may also be realistically increased. Bedtime, mealtime, and two additional times are reasonable for a small one, but limit each time to no longer than 5 minutes unless the child himself feels compelled to pray longer. Enforcing a strict time limit on prayer is not only unreasonable, it is counterproductive, for the child may begin to resent your control over his visits with God. Instead of one or two long prayer times, it is best to add three or four shorter times. Quality of prayer, not quantity of prayer, draws us nearer to the Lord; and this is the same for adults as for the children.

Main Idea to Be Presented

GOD IS FAITHFUL—he hears your prayers and he will always answer!

Taking your child's Bible, read to him, (on different days): John 11:41, 42; Matthew 7:7; John 14:13; and Jeremiah 33:3. Let your little one know that this is Jesus' assurance that God DOES hear his prayers and WILL answer his prayers because God is faithful. A wonderful way to explain the concept of faithfulness to a child is to liken God's faithfulness to his promises; a promise made by God is NEVER broken, and this is what being faithful is all about. Children understand promises far better than most adults and know well the shame and dishonesty of a broken promise!

Be prepared to field such delightful questions as "How can God hear me if he is in heaven?" or "If he can hear me talk, can he see me smile?" or even, "Will he call me on the telephone to answer my prayers?" Assure your child that God is all-powerful and is able to hear all prayers at the same time! Taking a cue from the telephone, your little one may understand more clearly how God hears prayer if he knows he has a **Hot Line to Heaven**! Like an invisible phone line from his heart of prayer to the Lord, he is able to visit with God anytime, day or night, without a busy signal or long distance telephone bill. (You may wish to refer to the activity section for 2- to 4-year-olds and share the **Hot Line to Heaven** activity.)

One-Step-Further Concept

Prayer has the power to heal through Jesus. Is there ever a five- or six-year-old without a scratch, scrape, or skinned something? Every child is able to relate to illness, injury, and hurt of both the body and the heart or the feelings. An astute parent will listen for clues as to the health-related conditions of family and friends of her child. Schoolmates may have chicken pox, teachers may call in substitutes, playmates may fall on their bicycles or skates. And this nearly endless list provides a marvelous avenue for helping your child to begin praying for others and seeing how the power of God can heal.

When there is a mention of illness or hurting hearts, suggest to your little one a prayer be offered for this person; that God loves all people and desires to see them healthy and happy. You may wish to refer to intercessory prayer as "prayer share"—sharing the love and help of Jesus with someone who may need his care. The heart of a five- or six-year-old is a sweet, tender heart which eagerly reaches out to embrace others. It nurtures their need to share God's protection and love when they offer up prayers in behalf of others.

**Now turn the page
to find fun activities
for teaching your
5- to 6-year-old to pray.**

Picture Prayer

You will need: small pieces of plain paper, crayons or markers

Suggested use:

Have your child draw, one at a time:

- 1 personal need
- 1 need of another person
- 1 "thank you" to God

Allow child to pray to the Father using the pictures to help her put needs and thanksgiving into words. A picture will often enable a small one to better vocalize what she feels! When you are finished with prayer time, paste the pictures to a large sheet of poster board entitled: I CARE THROUGH PRAYER. (*See picture below.*) Add to your collage whenever you use **Picture Prayers** and refer back to poster as you see God answering prayers to reinforce how God hears and answers prayer.

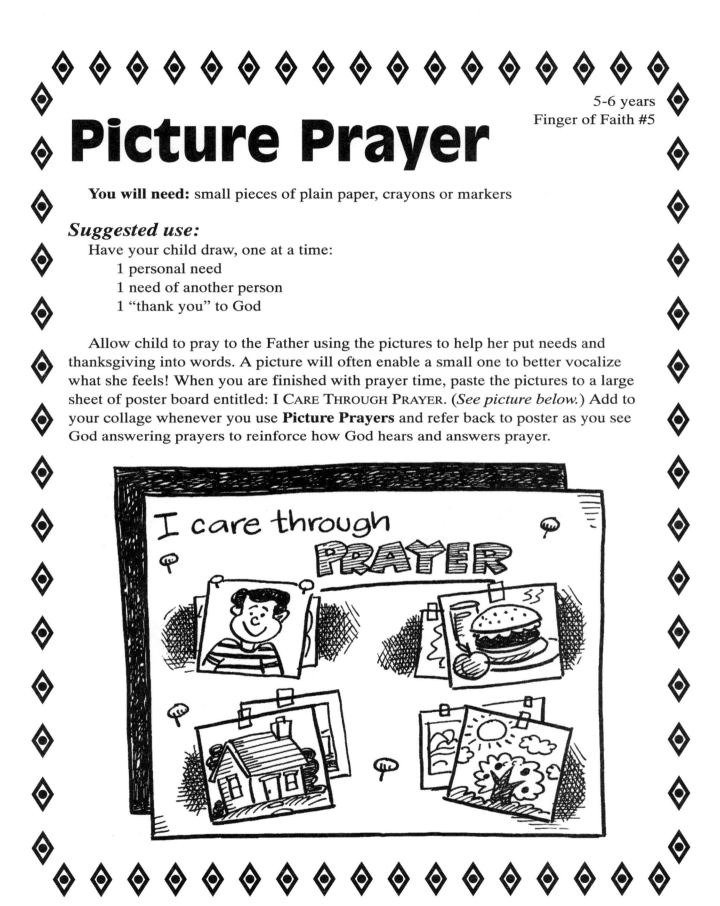

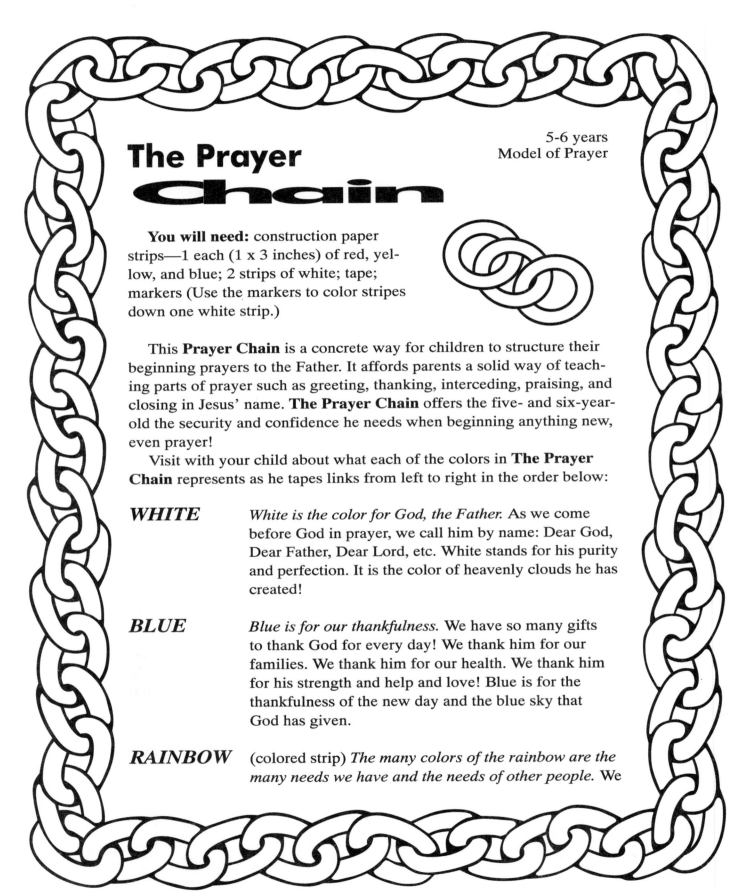

The Prayer Chain

You will need: construction paper strips—1 each (1 x 3 inches) of red, yellow, and blue; 2 strips of white; tape; markers (Use the markers to color stripes down one white strip.)

This **Prayer Chain** is a concrete way for children to structure their beginning prayers to the Father. It affords parents a solid way of teaching parts of prayer such as greeting, thanking, interceding, praising, and closing in Jesus' name. **The Prayer Chain** offers the five- and six-year-old the security and confidence he needs when beginning anything new, even prayer!

Visit with your child about what each of the colors in **The Prayer Chain** represents as he tapes links from left to right in the order below:

WHITE *White is the color for God, the Father.* As we come before God in prayer, we call him by name: Dear God, Dear Father, Dear Lord, etc. White stands for his purity and perfection. It is the color of heavenly clouds he has created!

BLUE *Blue is for our thankfulness.* We have so many gifts to thank God for every day! We thank him for our families. We thank him for our health. We thank him for his strength and help and love! Blue is for the thankfulness of the new day and the blue sky that God has given.

RAINBOW (colored strip) *The many colors of the rainbow are the many needs we have and the needs of other people.* We may need to ask the Lord to take away something we are afraid of or feel the need to ask him to help make our hearts happy. We may need to ask God to help a family member or friend who is sad or sick. Rainbows have many colors and we have many needs.

RED   *Red is for a heart of love!* In our prayers, we are able to tell God and Jesus and the Holy Spirit how much we love and need them. Just as we like to hear the words: "I love you," so God wants to hear "I love you," too. Red is a heart of love in prayer.

YELLOW   *Yellow is the color of the SON!* Because of Jesus' light and love, we are God's friends and can talk with God. We must always pray in the name of Jesus. When we end our prayers, we say, "In Jesus' name, amen." Yellow is for the sunshine love of Jesus!

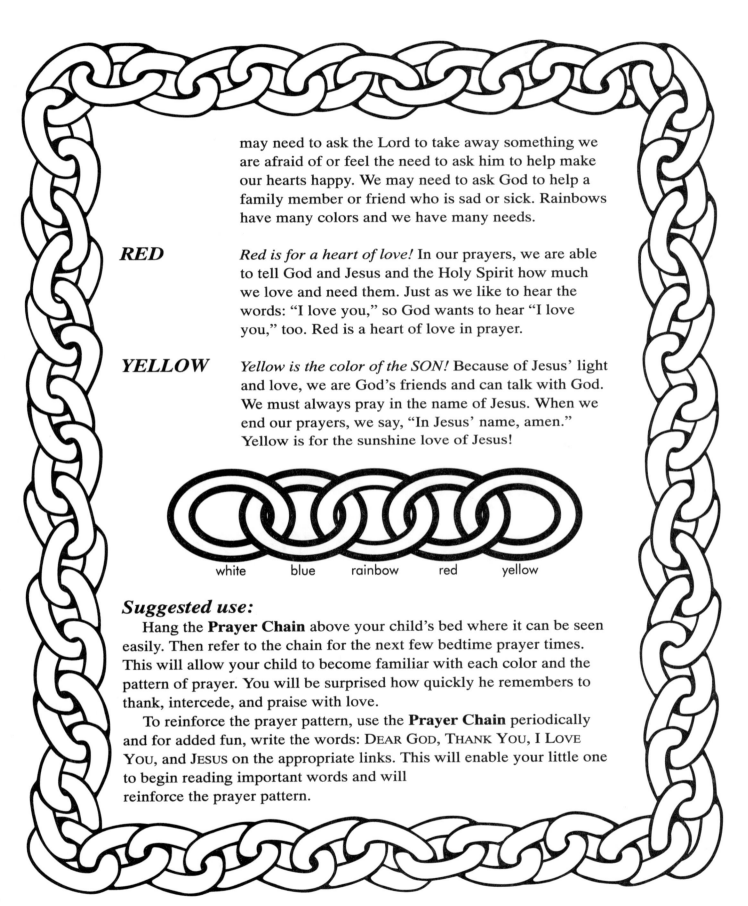

white   blue   rainbow   red   yellow

Suggested use:

Hang the **Prayer Chain** above your child's bed where it can be seen easily. Then refer to the chain for the next few bedtime prayer times. This will allow your child to become familiar with each color and the pattern of prayer. You will be surprised how quickly he remembers to thank, intercede, and praise with love.

To reinforce the prayer pattern, use the **Prayer Chain** periodically and for added fun, write the words: DEAR GOD, THANK YOU, I LOVE YOU, and JESUS on the appropriate links. This will enable your little one to begin reading important words and will reinforce the prayer pattern.

Prayer Share Teddy Bear

You will need: 1 small teddy bear, scraps of felt (red and any other colors), glue

Combine your child's imagination with your own to create **Prayer Share Teddy Bear**. Cut a small red felt heart and glue onto bear's body. Then make two felt bandages and glue them onto elbows or knees. Prepare tag from poster board. (*See pattern below.*) Personalize your prayer bear by adding ribbon, lace, buttons, hat, etc., if desired.

attach pieces with hot glue or fabric glue

Prayer Share Teddy Bear

use poster board

cut out of red felt

use any color felt and fine line permanent marker for making dots on bandages

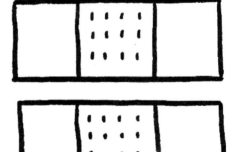

Prayer Share Teddy Bear, continued

Suggestions for use:

This is a good time to read 1 John 4:16 and visit with your child about how God loves each of us very, very much. When we love someone, we want to tell them how happy our heart is. (*Point to bear's heart.*) And if something hurts, we want to tell them about that too. (*Point to bandages on bear.*) Because God loves us, he wants to hear what our needs and wants are. He wants to hear us tell him we love him! God wants us to SHARE with him. (*Tell your child the bear's name: **Prayer Share Teddy Bear**.*) Allow child to cuddle the bear while he SHARES with God. The heart helps to remind your child of God's love and his love for God. Guide him to tell God of his love. The bandages help remind him of his own needs and the needs of others that can be shared with God. Guide your child to remember laying needs before God.

 PRAYER HANDS

You will need: hand pattern, white sheet of paper the same size as pattern, stapler, crayons

Color **God's Hands of Prayer** and then lay plain paper behind hand pattern and cut out 2 hands. Staple together on the guidelines, starting and stopping at the stars to leave opening.

Five- and six-year-olds often have difficulty expressing fear, loneliness and worry, which are common feelings that greatly increase as school begins, friendships expand, and independence is developed. The world is often a very intimidating and frightening place for this little believer of five or six and what a blessing to help your child learn early to place his cares in God's loving hands through prayer.

Suggested use:

Allow your child to draw or dictate so you can draw, on a small piece of paper, a fear or worry that may be bothering him. Visit about how Jesus is stronger than anyone or anything and because we belong to him, he will protect us and help us. We must give our fears and troubles to Jesus, and he will help.

Place picture inside of God's hands and pray together for the Lord's strength, love, and protection. If **Prayer Hands** are used at bedtime, when five- and six-year-old fears and worries are greatest, you may wish to place hands under pillow so your child knows God is at work even while he sleeps. You will be surprised at how well your little one will sleep, knowing his fears, etc., are literally in the hands of the Lord!

God's
Hands
of
Prayer

Prayer Pillow

Every parent knows how readily his child accepts and cuddles a favorite, beloved stuffed teddy bear, rag doll or love-worn blanket! There is something about the nonjudgmental attitude of a teddy bear that fosters genuine love and trust in a little one and allows him to open up and express feelings more completely.

Using a fluffy **Prayer Pillow** is another way of providing your child with the feeling of physical security. Allow him to help you design his special **Prayer Pillow.** If you are a seamstress, this should be delightfully simple. However most of us need to purchase a plain ready-made pillow which may be simply decorated. Using buttons, ribbons, fabric paint or whatever, allow your child time to create a pillow he will wish to hold and cuddle as he prays to his Father. Let your child know he is making this special pillow for the Lord and will present it to him along with his prayers and thanksgiving.

The **Prayer Pillow** is a loving reminder of prayerful chats with God; a pretty addition to your little one's room or bed; an enjoyable gift to the Lord. It is a secure, only-to-be-shared-with-Jesus way of holding prayer close to the heart.

Open-Your-♡ Prayer

You will need: a heart shaped box (*Valentine candy box is perfect.*) or any box decorated with hearts (*must have lid*)

Suggested use:

Visit with your child about how God, because he loves your child so, wants to know what is in his heart. And sometimes we must be very still and quiet to hear and see what is deep inside our hearts.

Hand your child the closed heart box. Ask him to be very quiet and still for a few moments to look deep inside his heart for what he will say to God. (*These seconds of silence may be a challenge at first, but hang in there!*) Now allow child to open his heart (*the box*) and to talk with God.

Many children will prefer to open their hearts to the Lord in a private way without the parent nearby. This may be a good time to visit the rest room or check on another blanket to give your child time alone with the Lord.

God Heard Me Today

Place a sticker or draw a star in each box under the days you pray to your Father.

5-6 years

Sunday	Monday	Tuesday	Wednesday	Thursday	Friday	Saturday

When a ♡ tugs, GOD hugs!

Color in a heart for each day you pray to your Father.

Pray every day!

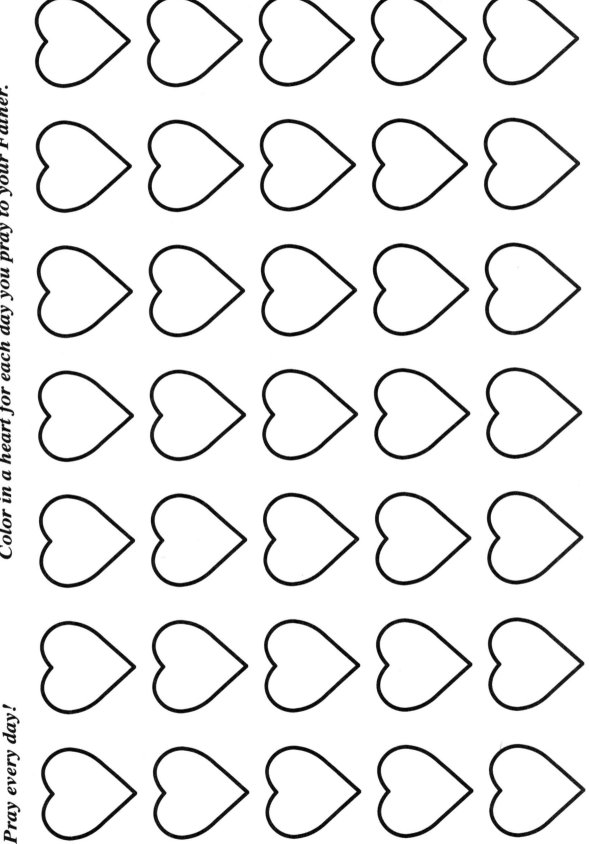

Echo Prayer

This prayer style helps your child, through example, to know how to pray to the Father. Modeling his prayer from the parent, but using his own words, your five- or six-year-old will gain prayer confidence and be greatly enriched through the sharing of prayer.

Suggested use:

The parent begins by greeting God and then pausing to allow child to echo style, but use his own, different words. For example:

Parent: "Dear heavenly Father ..." (pause)

Child: "Dear God ..." (pause)

(*Prayer continues in same "echo" method.*)

Parent: "Thank you for our family's happiness ..." (pause)

Child: "Thank you for Jimmy who is my friend ..." (pause)

Parent: "Please help me be a better listener ..." (pause)

Child: "Please help me not to fight with my sister ..." (pause)

Parent: "I give you my heart, Jesus ..." (pause)

Child: "I love you, Jesus ..." (pause)

Parent: "In Jesus' name we pray, amen."

Child: "In Jesus' name, amen."

Echo Prayer is a good time to share Matthew 18:19, 20 with your little one; that when two or more pray together in the name of Jesus, he is with them and this is a gift from God. Prayers prayed with others who love Jesus have great power to help and heal!

Praying With Your 7-10 Year Old

Characteristics

If curiosity is the key ingredient in the small child, and exploration in the beginning scholar, then reasoning is the benchmark for middle-aged children of seven to ten years. No longer content with how things work, they hunger to know *why* things work the way they do. A mixture of expanded vocabulary, personal experience, and independent thinking interweave to create a hungry mind, voraciously seeking to understand the *why*'s of everything—including prayer! This is the beginning of true analytical reasoning and opens wide the door for delightful discussions about the Lord and his awesome power and love.

Though your child is at an age where independent thinking is unfurling around her like a flag of freedom, age has also begun to clip the wings of childlike spontaneity. Your daughter begins to think and reason more before acting and before sharing her feelings. What a two-edged sword! When the wonders of independent reasoning begin to blossom, the perceived judgments of others sprout painful thorns which poke at her confidence, and spontaneous creativity and expression begin the process of withering.

Afraid she will "do it all wrong" or others may laugh, your child may shy away from sharing emotions, especially in verbal prayer. Some parents may feel twinges of hurt when their once open child no longer readily confides in them. Recognize and respect her need for privacy, but encourage her to share with God. It is nice when our children confide in us, but it is life giving when they freely confide in their heavenly Father!

Peers have stolen center stage with the seven- to ten-year-old, turning his world into a social frenzy of classroom friends, fun, and foes. From peer praise to peer pain, your child's class-mates wield the power of a thou-sand Supreme Court judges! Peer pain has the amazing power to turn the very shoes your son dreamed of owning into a vile curse upon his feet should his classmates turn in the wrong verdict of style. Conversely, peer praise has few equals in lifting the morale. Just notice the jaunty swing in your daughter's ponytail the next time she is peer compli-mented on her poem or new hair bow!

Peer power has incredibly strong sway but is only a wispy shadow in light of God's might, and your child needs to be reminded of this often. Gently guide him to realize that earthly judgment by peers is as dust; it will blow away and be for-gotten tomorrow. Only the Word of the Lord and his truth are everlasting, and God does not judge by appearances but by the condition of the heart. Share 1 Samuel 16:7 aloud with your child and thank the Lord, through your prayers, that our Father looks at the goodness inside of us instead of at our clothes or hair. (See **Present Prayers: Bullies, Praise, and Worries** for more encouragement.)

> "If God heard my prayer, where is his answer?"
>
> **Neal, age 9**

Suggested Prayer Times

Bedtime, mealtime, and three addition-al moments of prayer give your child short time-outs and longer refreshment-learning times with the Lord. Again, pre-sent your prayer lesson at one of these times and be flexible with your timing. Walk softly, as you are entering the seven- to ten-year-old *time bomb field!* With more school work, music lessons, sports, and social activi-ties, your child's day is fairly bursting, and any restrictions you place on his time may be cause for a blowup. Be careful that prayer is not mis-understood as a free time activity. Instead it is a life sustaining need. Present prayer as time spent with your child's best friend and Father.

The concept of "3 minute devotions" may ease your child gracefully into spending more time in prayer. Three minute devotions are those little times your child can spend asking God's help with friend troubles in the gym or those moments of thankfulness and praise for teacher's patience with that overdue pro-ject. Assure your child that anytime we come before the Lord, whether it is a 3 minute devotion in the stillness of the school rest room or the half hour before bed, it is prayer. There is simply no time requirement in prayer; it is the condition of the heart and our faithfulness in turning to the Lord that provides strength through prayer.

Main Idea to Be Presented

God hears and answers prayer—in his time and in his will.

What a mighty and often frustrating lesson this is for children to learn; and yet once digested, it will usher in a new, deeper level of Godly trust, perseverance, and patience in prayer.

Allow your child to help recount the story of Joshua and the victory at Jericho. Point out the miraculous way in which God chose to bring Joshua and his chosen people into the city of Jericho. Can your child think of any other ways Joshua might have entered the city? (*Through gates, window openings, over the top of the walls, etc.*) Ask him whether he thinks Joshua expected God to do what he did. God certainly worked in his own way and in his own time at Jericho, and this is how God always works!

Answers to prayer may be sometimes surprising, often miraculous, but always faithful. Read aloud Jeremiah 33:3; Psalm 91:15; Isaiah 65:24; Luke 11:9 and John 15:7. God promises to hear our prayers and to answer each one if we pray in the name of Jesus Christ.

Share Ecclesiastes 3:1, 11. Though God does promise an answer to every prayer, he does not use an earthly time schedule. And his answer may not always be what we had hoped. Guide your child to see that a loving father will not give something to his child if it is bad for him (Matthew 7:9-11), and because God loves us above all else, he will only give to us what we ask if what we desire is truly best. When we lay our needs at his feet, it is up to us to be patient for his answer, and then accept, with thankfulness, his provision.

Help your child to see how God answers faithful prayer by using the **Prayer Log** in the activity section for seven- to ten-year-olds. By noting when he prayed and for what/whom he prayed, your child will be able to see when God faithfully answers his prayers. What a joyous testimony his **Prayer Log** will be with time. (*Be sure to encourage your child to pray continually for his needs as it states in 1 Thessalonians 5:17, "Pray continually."*)

One-Step-Further Concept

Help your child to memorize James 4:7, "Submit yourselves, then, to God. Resist the devil, and he will flee from you." Lead him to see that this is God's command to us for his divine protection against Satan and his evil. We must:

1. Submit to God. (*Prayer to the Father is submission.*)
2. Resist the devil. (*Prayer draws us to God whom Satan fears.*)
3. He will flee. (*Satan cannot be near those who are near to God in prayer!*)

Allow your child to read Ephesians 6:10-18; John 17:11; and 1 Peter 5:8, 9. Discuss with him any fears, questions, or concerns he may have about Satan while reassuring him that God-given prayer has the power to protect. (*Refer to **Prayer Warrior** in the activity section.*)

> **Now turn the page to find fun activities for teaching your 7- to 10-year-old to pray.**

Daily Prayer ROCKETS

Your LOVE to God!

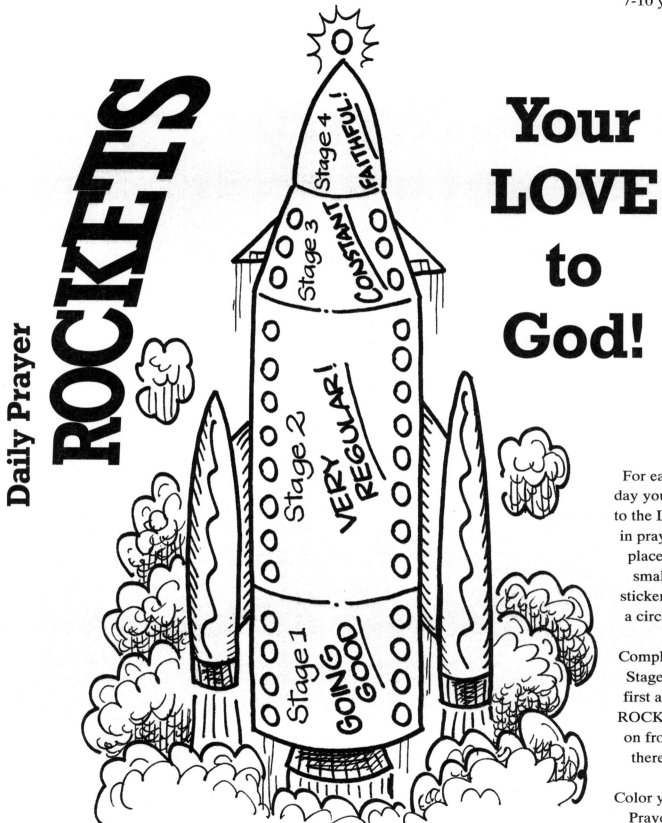

For each day you go to the Lord in prayer, place a small sticker in a circle.

Complete Stage 1 first and ROCKET on from there!

Color your Prayer Rocket.

Prayers!

You will need: 1 empty can, construction paper, glue, markers, (glitter, sequins, etc., if desired)

This prayer lesson on God's strength and the strengthening power of prayer is ideal to use when your child is bitten by the "I can't" bug. Read aloud Philippians 4:13 and 2 Corinthians 12:9, 10 while you visit about the big God we serve. He is bigger than any problem, any person, or any thing; and if we serve him faithfully and give our weaknesses and fears to him, he will "can" any obstacles in our lives!

Help your child to recognize that "I can'ts" are only Satan's lies to pull our faith away from God and make us even weaker. When we feel as if we can't, *God can do* it all!

Allow your child to create a fabulous, new label for his own GOD CAN-DO can using construction paper and decorations. On the front write: GOD CAN-DO and on the back write: So I CAN, TOO! *(See illustration.)*

front

back

While you work, be sure to share a few of your own testimonies of times God turned you into a can-do creation through your prayers.

Suggestions for use:

Before prayer time, allow time for both you and your child to write an "I can't" worry on a slip of paper. Drop them into the GOD CAN-DO can. Encourage your child to verbalize his need for strength during prayer. When we verbalize our need, it humbles our hearts before the Lord and allows God to work powerfully to strengthen us. Periodically pull out the slips of paper and share your testimonies of how God helped you both become "can-do"ers through your prayer.

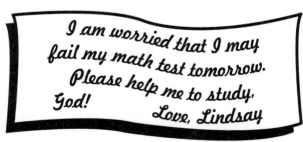

I am worried that I may fail my math test tomorrow. Please help me to study, God!
Love, Lindsay

Let Go and Let God Prayers

You will need: 1 piece of poster board (2 feet x 2 feet), 5 rubber bands, markers

This particular prayer lesson teaches that God's will shall be done, if we let go of our selfishness, our fears and worries, and anything else that holds us tightly bound. Only then will God step in to do mighty works in our lives. Our prayers can ask God to help us LET GO and LET HIM WORK!

Have your child stretch out a rubber band and hold it tautly, while you say: "This rubber band is like our life when something negative is holding onto us—something like fear or doubt or jealousy or anger. These kinds of feelings keep us from doing God's work. They weaken our faith and smother the joy that God has placed in our hearts. When something or someone has such a hold on us, we don't allow God to work his will in our lives.

We must pray and ask God to help us let go of things that we allow to hold him back. Nothing must stop us from doing his will or praying or loving through him. *(Read the last part of 1 Peter 3:7, ". . . so that nothing will hinder your prayers.")*

Our prayers help us to LET GO . . . *(Have your child let the rubber band fly!)* . . . and LET GOD work his will in our lives. *(Read aloud Philippians 2:13.)*

Encourage your child to verbalize the things, feelings, or people he feels may be holding him back and to pray for God's strength in helping him follow God with his whole being.

Game time!   *Game time!*

You can make a fun game for both of you to play now. Use the illustration below to create a target board. Cut the center hole out and set your board on a table, leaning against the wall. Take turns, at varying distances, shooting the rubber bands through the bull's-eye. SCORE: 50 points for each bull's-eye. First one to reach 500 wins!

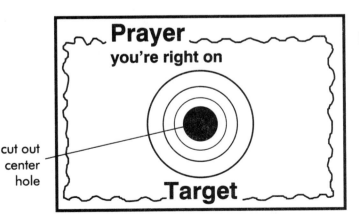

poster board

Prayer
you're right on

cut out
center
hole

Target

No need for . . .

Rabbit Foot Faith

You will need: 1 sheet of white typing paper, markers, stapler, scissors, facial tissues, rabbit pattern

One of the most powerful promises God makes to us in our faithful prayer is that he will hear and answer us. We do not need to use "rabbit's foot faith," but rather, radical expectancy.

Visit with your child about those times when it may seem as if God has not heard her prayers or has not answered them. Read aloud Jeremiah 33:3, Psalm 91:15, and Isaiah 65:24. God has promised he will hear our prayers and answer each one, but will do it in his own time and in his own way. Explain how his answer may not be the one we had wanted nor in the time frame we envisioned. Nevertheless, GOD WILL ANSWER PRAYER.

Ask your child to name any good luck charms she is able to think of *(for example: rabbit's feet, horse shoes, clovers, etc.)*. Tell her these are lies to keep us from putting our whole faith in God's promises. When we ask anything in the name of Jesus, it will be given. *(Read Matthew 7:7 and John 16:24)* With prayer and our faith in God's promises, we have no need of rabbit foot faith or hope—we have the spirit of radical expectancy.

Make the stuffed rabbit to have some fun reinforcing the concept that God does hear and answer faithful prayer.

Directions:

1. Color rabbit.
2. Lay sheet of typing paper behind rabbit pattern and carefully cut out the rabbit. (You will have two rabbits cut!)
3. Staple the two rabbits at each dash. Be sure to stop and start at the dots, but DO NOT staple between them!

4. Stuff facial tissues into the rabbit at the opening. Make him a fluffy, plump bunny!
5. Now staple the opening closed and you are finished.

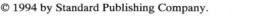

I need my foot to HOP-
to help me run 'n LOPE...
But YOU don't need a
rabbit's foot,
'CUZ
JESUS
is YOUR HOPE!"

"Ask and you will receive,
and your joy will be complete."
John 16:24

The Prayer Warrior

You will need: roll of aluminum foil

Ask your child if he realizes that he is a soldier—a warrior of God! Explain how we are engaged every day in a battle of good versus evil. We fight against temptation, sin, lies, gossip, hurtful thoughts and words, and we don't love the Lord as we should. Read 1 Timothy 6:12 aloud and discuss how faithful prayers can help us fight the good fight. Now read Ephesians 6:10-18 and see if your child can locate the six pieces of God's shiny armor.

Using the aluminum foil, allow your child to sculpt himself as God's **Prayer Warrior** who is fighting the good fight through the power of mighty prayer! Be sure to have your child sculpt the six pieces of the armor of God as part of his statue. As you work, visit about prayer as a holy weapon; how our daily prayers strengthen us in the name of Jesus and even help strengthen others for whom we pray. *(This is a good time to introduce or review the concept of intercession.)*

Set your **Prayer Warrior** beside the bed as a reminder to your child to pray the full armor of God as protection every day. Ephesians 6:18 is a powerful command that we should pray on all occasions and for all God's people; that if we are faithful in prayer to the heavenly Father, we will be able to stand against all the forces of evil with God's strength. Victory is ours in the Lord!

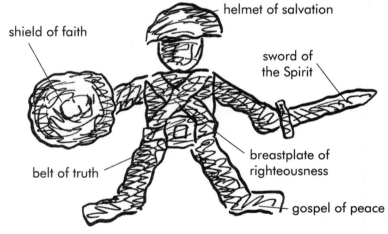

shield of faith
helmet of salvation
sword of the Spirit
belt of truth
breastplate of righteousness
gospel of peace

Here are additional Scripture verses to share with your child. Take turns reading them aloud and write your child's favorite verse on an index card. Set it in front of the **Prayer Warrior** and challenge your child to memorize this "weapon" in one night. If he repeats it the next night, make a new challenge card. How many "weapons" is your warrior able to collect?

* James 5:13   * Luke 22:40   * 2 Samuel 22:33
* James 4:7   * Isaiah 41:10   * Ephesians 6:10

Present Prayers

You will need: colored ribbons (in lengths of 6 inches), wrapping paper, (6 x 8 inches), permanent marker, copies of prayers, old wallpaper book (or 11 by 16 inch piece)

Before first use of Present Prayers:

Cut apart prayers on following pages and roll them up in wrapping paper. Tie with a ribbon. You may wish to keep track of which prayer is in each wrapper by attaching a small tag identifying subject. *(Examples: fears, parents, etc.)* Place all wrapped prayers but one in a bag. You will be pulling them out, as desired, at those times you wish to "gift" your child with a special prayer.

Present Prayers are an answer to a child's need to see how prayers can be put into words for various situations and needs, including intercessory prayer. The prayers in this section act as an example for your child at those times he wants to pray for a particular thing but is not sure how to place his request before the throne of God. These prayers also help broaden the ways your child can address the Lord and how Scripture may be prayed.

Suggestion for use:

Tell your child his prayers are like presents from his heart to the Father. *(Hold up a wrapped Present Prayer.)* We all have needs; we all feel hurt; we all worry. Yet sometimes we are at a loss as to how to put these feelings into words.

Present your child with the wrapped **Present Prayer.** Allow him to open it up and to read it aloud. Tell him that every so often, you will "gift" him with a **Present Prayer** that may help him put needs into words of prayer. Tonight he is going to make a special book cover so he can collect and keep each **Present Prayer** as it is received. He will then have a whole collection of prayers to refer to whenever needed.

How to make book cover:

Have your child choose a piece of wallpaper he likes in the wallpaper book. Cut it out. Fold it in half and, using the marker, title it **PRESENT PRAYERS.** Decorate if you wish. Slide the first **Present Prayer** into the folder and keep the folder handy for sliding in more when they are given. After all 12 have been collected, staple booklet together.

Present Prayers (cut apart)

FOR WORRIES ABOUT SCHOOL

Food for thought: God is with me *everywhere.*
Key Verse: "Who of you by worrying can add a single hour to his life?" (Matthew 6:27).

Dear heavenly Father,
    I thank you that you are always with me throughout my days and nights. You walk with me even as I go through my day at school and you know the problems, worries, and joys of all my classes, teachers, and friends.
    Lord, I have some worries in school about *(name)* and I ask your help in solving these problems in the way you would best do. Help me to keep my eyes on you and not on worries. You are mightier than anything in this world; you are bigger than my worries!
    I love you, Father. You are my strength, and my faith lives in you alone.
    In Jesus' name, amen.

(READ: Matthew 6:25, 26; Psalm 147:5)

FREEDOM FROM FEAR

Food for thought: Faith can melt away any fears.
Key Verse: "Surely God is my salvation; I will trust and not be afraid. The Lord, the Lord, is my strength and my song" (Isaiah 12:2).

Dear Lord God,
    You are mighty above all things in Heaven and on earth. You can win any battle; and with you, I can overcome any fear! Father, I am afraid of *(name)* and I ask for your love and strength to melt away this fear. Because I belong to you, I know you will protect me and never leave me alone to face what I am afraid of. You will be with me and take these fears far from me!
    I thank you, Lord, for being bigger than any of my fears. My strength comes from you. I will sing of your strength in my heart.
    In the name of Jesus I pray, amen.

(READ: Psalm 27:1; Joshua 1:9)

DEALING WITH A BULLY

Food for thought: Give a bully to God with love.
Key Verse: "But I tell you: Love your enemies and pray for those who persecute you" (Matthew 5:44).

Dear Mighty Lord,
    You alone are God over all Heaven and earth. All strength is in your hands. You have the greatest power to conquer and you have the greatest power to love and forgive.
    Father, I am having trouble dealing with *(name)*. Your word tells me to love my enemy. Please help my heart be willing to love *(name)* even when he bothers me so! Help me to try and understand why he acts this way and to forgive him.
    In the forgiving name of Jesus I pray, amen.

REJOICING IN THE LORD

Food for thought: Prayer can be a song of praise and joy.
Key Verse: "Sing to him, sing praise to him; tell of all his wonderful acts" (Psalm 105:2).

Dear Abba Father, *(Abba means most loving Father)*
My heart is filled with love for all you have done for me and all that you are going to do in my life. I can feel your great love every day. I want to share with many others the peace, joy, and happiness you have given me. I will tell them of your power and promises. I will do things for them with a smile. I will sing praises to you all the time.
Thank you, Lord, for loving me as your child. I want to love you with all my heart, soul and strength.
In Jesus' name, amen.

(READ: Deuteronomy 6:5-8; Psalm 113)

FOR FAMILY PEACE

Food for thought: God can mend and strengthen families.
Key Verse: "He heals the brokenhearted and binds up their wounds" (Psalm 147:3).

Dear Lord God,
You are all loving and all merciful. You heal hurt bodies and can mend the broken hearts in people, too. Father, our family's heart is hurting. We forget the love you pour out and want us to share with our family so that we can be strong in you.
Please touch our hurting family, Lord, and help us to mend back together. Your power and your promises offer peace and strength and love. I put my hope in you, Father, and know you are the healer of whole families.
In the name of Jesus, amen.

(READ: Psalm 145:18; Matthew 18:20)

FOR MY PARENTS

Food for thought: Parents are a special gift from God.
Key Verse: "Children, obey your parents in the Lord, for this is right" (Ephesians 6:1).

Dear Father,
You are my heavenly Father and you protect me and teach me. You help me when I am hurt and love me no matter what I may do. My parents try to do the same in their great love for me. I thank you, Lord, for choosing the parents you have for me.
Please help me to obey them even when it is hard. You gave us commandments to live by because you love us. Help me to understand that my parents' rules are because they love me and want to protect me.
Keep them safe, dear Lord, as they go about their day, and help me to remember to say thank you for all they have given and all they do for me.
In Jesus' name I pray, amen.

FOR MY BROTHER/SISTER

Food for thought: How lonely you would be without a brother/sister to love.
Key Verse: "Keep on loving each other as brothers" (Hebrews 13:1).

Dear Lord,
  You sent your only Son, Jesus, to be my Savior and my brother. I thank you for my brother Jesus and I thank you for my brother/sister *(name)*. I love her very much even though sometimes I do not show it.
  Help me, Father, to be more understanding, patient and giving to *(name)*. Please help me to love and treat *(name)* just as I would my brother Jesus.
  In the name of my brother Jesus I pray, amen.

(READ: 1 John 4:7; James 1:19)

FOR A TROUBLED FRIEND

Food for thought: Having true friends is a big responsibility.
Key Verse: "Greater love has no one than this, that he lay down his life for his friends" (John 15:13).

Dear heavenly God,
  Your word tells how your love covers everyone; and you have taught me to love and pray for my friends when they are in need. I am worried about *(name)*, Father. His heart is very troubled and he needs your strength and love to protect him.
  I ask you to help *(name)* put his eyes upon you, Lord, and hold onto your strength and love. Let him know that you are bigger than any troubles.
  Lord, help me to be a true friend; to be encouraging and to help lead *(name)* back to you.
  In Jesus' name, amen.

(READ: Proverbs 17:17; Ecclesiastes 4:10)

FORGIVING OTHERS

Food for thought: Forgiveness clears our hearts to love God more.
Key Verse: "Bear with each other and forgive whatever grievances you may have against one another. Forgive as the Lord forgave you" (Colossians 3:13).

Dear Father in Heaven,
  Your mercy and forgiveness are as deep as your love. It is because of the mighty love in your heart that we have been forgiven through Jesus. Lord, please help me to have a loving heart big enough to forgive other people for what they may do or say to hurt me. You tell us we are to forgive over and over again and not keep count. Help me be willing to do this.
  I thank you especially, Father, that Jesus forgave us and does not carry a grudge. It is because of Jesus' forgiveness that I can be your friend, God. Let me have a forgiving heart so that I, too, may be forgiven.
  In the precious name of Jesus I pray, amen.

(READ: Ephesians 4:32; Mark 11:25; Luke 17:4)

FOR STRENGTH TO SAY: NO!

Food for thought: Satan wants you to say YES; God's strength will help you say NO!

Key Verse: "Because he himself suffered when he was tempted, he is able to help those who are being tempted" (Hebrews 2:18).

Dear Mighty Lord God,

I praise you for your great strength. YOU are champion and victor over all Heaven and earth! I know, Lord, when I rely on you for strength, you will make me strong.

I am feeling temptation, Father, over _____ and I need your help to say NO. I know you understand how I feel and you have promised to show me the way to stand bravely against any temptation.

Temptation is not from you, Lord God, but winning strength to say NO is! Help me stand strong in you, Lord, and to resist temptation. Strengthen me to just say NO!

In the powerful name of Jesus, amen.

(READ: James 4:7; 2 Samuel 22:33; Psalm 28:7)

FOR WALKING NEARER WITH GOD

Food for thought: If you are not seeking God, you are lost.

Key Verse: "Look to the Lord and his strength; seek his face always" (Psalm 105:4).

Dear Lord God Jehovah, *(Jehovah means only true God)*
I am so happy that you are always with me, but I must confess that sometimes I do not keep my eyes upon you. I become busy with things and forget that you are all that truly matters. You want so much to talk with me; to share my feelings; to hold me. Father, please help me to remember you love me more than anyone else loves me. Help me to always seek your loving face with all my heart and know that you are not the one who wanders away from me. I am the one who wanders from you.

Lord, I love you, and I am lost when I wander. I want to be nearer to you every day.
In Jesus' name, amen.

(READ: Hebrews 12:2; Isaiah 55:6; Psalm 27:8)

FOR ILLNESS/HEALING

Food for thought: Prayer is the best medicine.

Key Verse: "'But I will restore you to health and heal your wounds,' declares the Lord" (Jeremiah 30:17).

Dear Lord God,

I thank you that you alone are the God who heals us. You want us to have happy and healthy hearts, minds, and bodies so we can serve you.

I ask you, Lord, to heal *(name)* of *(illness/hurt)*. I care for and love *(name),* but know you love him even more. You tell us to love and offer prayers for those who are hurting or ill, Father. I know that you hear my prayers.

Help me to understand that you heal in many ways, Lord, and help me to be patient. With you, all things are possible and I pray that *(name)* be healed in your way and in your time.

In Jesus' loving name, amen.

(READ: James 5:16; Exodus 15:26; Psalm 103:3)

The PRAYER LETTER

You will need: pencil or pen, Prayer Letter

This double prayer lesson may be done in one night or turned into a two night lesson. Through using this **Prayer Letter** lesson, your child should gain greater confidence and understand the model of prayer that Jesus offered us in the Lord's Prayer. You will want to have a Bible handy, marked at Matthew 6:9-13 and John 16:24.

PART 1 *Jesus' Spoken Prayer Letter*

Your child has been learning the parts of a letter in English class at school. Ask him to identify the three main parts of a letter: the *greeting,* the *body,* and the *closing.* Tell your child that Jesus gave us a beautiful prayer—a verbal love letter to God—that contains the same parts as a letter.

Open your Bible to Matthew 6:9-13 and have your child read the Lord's Prayer aloud. Now ask him if he is able to identify the *greeting,* the *body,* and the *closing. (You will have to help him with the closing, for it is in John 16:24.)*

Help your child see that we address God by name in the *greeting;* that we offer him praise and thanks and lay our needs and the needs of others before him in the *body;* and that we always *close* our prayers with praise and in the name of Jesus.

Now move to the top half of the next page.

PART 2 *A Love Letter to God*

You have seen how the prayer Jesus prayed in Matthew 6:9-13 *(and in Luke 11:2-4)* is like a verbal love letter to our Father. This is what prayer really is; it is composing a letter from your heart and in your heart to the Lord.

Ask your child whether he remembers the first time he ever wrote a letter to a friend or pen pal. Was it hard to think of what to say? Did he find that after he wrote a few letters and grew closer to his friend, the letters became much easier to write?

It is the same with prayer. If your child uses the **Prayer Letter** and its three parts (*greeting, body,* and *closing*), it will help him think of what to say to God, and after a while, he will be praying and visiting with the Father with the same ease he has in talking to friends and family he loves most.

Use the spaces on the bottom half of the next page to write a **Prayer Letter** to the Lord. Decorate your stationery and be sure to use the *greeting,* the *body,* and the *closing.* See whether you are able to use at least 5 of the following words somewhere in your letter.

> *forgive, holy, Jesus, thankful, love, strengthen, beautiful, need, glorious, help, blessings, healing*

Prayer Letter Activity

PART 1. Fill in the blanks to the Lord's Prayer (Matthew 6:9-14, NIV).
Then circle the parts to the prayer as stated on the right.

"OUR _____ IN _____, _____ BE
YOUR _____, YOUR _____ COME,
YOUR WILL BE DONE ON _____ AS IT IS
IN _____. GIVE US TODAY OUR DAILY
_____. FORGIVE US OUR _____, AS
WE ALSO HAVE FORGIVEN OUR _____.
AND LEAD US NOT INTO _____, BUT
DELIVER US FROM THE _____
_____."
IN THE NAME OF _____, AMEN.

| Circle the GREETING in red. |
| Circle the BODY in yellow (praise/needs). |
| Circle the CLOSING in blue (from John 16:24). |

Greeting   **Body (praise, needs, thanks)**   **Closing**

Dear

My Prayer Log

Date	Prayed for	Scripture read
_____	_____	_____
_____	_____	_____
_____	_____	_____
_____	_____	_____
_____	_____	_____
_____	_____	_____
_____	_____	_____
_____	_____	_____
_____	_____	_____
_____	_____	_____
_____	_____	_____
_____	_____	_____
_____	_____	_____
_____	_____	_____

In His Name

Even though these are the last pages in this book, I hope you feel it is really the beginning: the beginning of a wondrous time of sharing precious prayer with your child; the beginning of a prayerful life of growing intimacy between your child and our heavenly Father. The beauty in this beginning is that it has no end. It is not a particular prayer we seek to give our little ones, but rather a prayerful life-style, continually drawing nearer to the Lord from each "Dear Father" to every "amen." We are nurturing our own prayers that the children we hold in the center of our love will reflexively turn to the Lord at all times throughout their lives, for his strength, his overcoming victory, his faithful companionship, and his abundant love!

Whether it is the leap from toddler to youth, the stretch from youth to teen, or the awkward struggle of teen turning adult, our children need our help in seeking the Lord through prayer. And we have precious little time; for one day, we will turn around and quite suddenly, our little ones will be grown and have children and adult problems of their own. It is the prayerful life-style we nurture today that will keep them on the sustaining path of God tomorrow.

This then, is our one, true living legacy of love: the only gift we will give to our children that "no thief comes near and no moth destroys" (Luke 12:33 NIV). The prayer life we teach and nurture now will radiantly live on between Father and child forever!

So, let us teach our children the Word of God. Let us teach them of Jesus' love and salvation. And let us teach our children the glorious beauty of daily prayer that will set their feet firmly and forever on the rock of God!

THE PRAYER ROCK

(A fun activity for you and your child to share.)

You will need:
- 2 smooth, medium-sized rocks
- 2 squares of brightly patterned fabric *(6 inches by 6 inches each)*
- 2 ribbon ties *(each 6 inches long)*
- 2 rubber bands

Directions:
1. Lay rock on center of fabric, print side down.
2. Pull corners up to meet at top and gather fabric around rock.
3. Wind rubber band around "neck" of fabric.
4. Tie ribbon bow over rubber band.

Now read the poem on the next page to see what your **Prayer Rock** can do for you! These make lovely gifts for grandparents or friends. Be sure to include a copy of the poem with your gift.

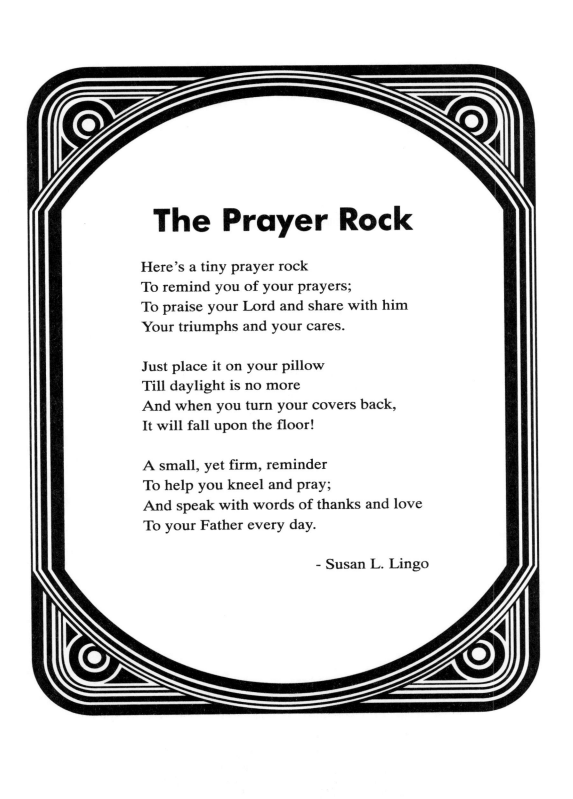

The Prayer Rock

Here's a tiny prayer rock
To remind you of your prayers;
To praise your Lord and share with him
Your triumphs and your cares.

Just place it on your pillow
Till daylight is no more
And when you turn your covers back,
It will fall upon the floor!

A small, yet firm, reminder
To help you kneel and pray;
And speak with words of thanks and love
To your Father every day.

- Susan L. Lingo